The Modern Spanish Novel 1898–1936

Twayne's World Authors Series

Spanish Literature

Janet Pérez, Editor

Texas Tech University

TWAS 764

The Modern Spanish Novel 1898–1936

By Ricardo Landeira

University of Wyoming

Twayne Publishers • *Boston*

The Modern Spanish
Novel 1898–1936

Ricardo Landeira

Book Production by Lyda E. Kuth
Book Design by Barbara Anderson

Printed on permanent/durable acid-free
paper and bound in the United States of
America.

**Library of Congress Cataloging in
Publication Data**

Landeira, Ricardo, 1944–
    The modern Spanish novel, 1898–1936.

    (Twayne's world author series ; TWAS 764. Spanish
literature)
    Bibliography: p. 148
    1. spanish fiction—20th century—History and
criticism. I. Title. II. Series: Twayne's world
author series ; TWAS 764. III. Series: Twayne's
world author series. Spanish literature.
PQ6144.L36 1985   863'.62'09   85–7678
ISBN 0–8057–6603–0

For Joy

Contents

About the Author

Professor Ricardo Landeira was born in El Ferrol del Caudillo, Spain, but received his university education in the United States. He holds the B.A. and M.A. from Arizona State University, and the Ph.D. from Indiana University with a combined specialization in Spanish and comparative literature.

He has taught at Arizona State University and Duke University, was Fulbright Lecturer at the University of Santiago de Compostela, and is presently at the University of Wyoming.

Professor Landeira's areas of specialization are nineteenth- and twentieth-century peninsular Spanish literature. His critical works to date include *Gabriel Miró: Trilogía de Sigüenza*, *An Annotated Bibliography of Gabriel Miró (1900–1978)*, *Critical Essays on Gabriel Miró*, *Ignacio Aldecoa: A Collection of Critical Essays* (in collaboration); *Ramiro de Maeztu*, and *José de Espronceda*. He has published many articles in the areas of nineteenth- and twentieth-century poetry and fiction, these essays appearing in such journals as *Revista Hispánica Moderna*, *Romance Notes*, *Boletín de la Real Academia Española*, *Journal of Spanish Studies: Twentieth Century*, *Anales de la narrativa española contemporánea*, *Cuadernos Hispanoamericanos*, and *Insula*. Prominent among several research projects is a book on the theme of incest in Spanish literature.

Preface

This genre volume is concerned with the novels of two generations whose works appeared approximately between 1898 and 1936. Curiously enough, neither of the two dates has a strictly literary significance, though both figure prominently in most histories, anthologies, and other Spanish literature texts. The years 1898 and 1936 represent, instead, signposts in the political history of Spain that bring to mind disastrous conflicts most Spaniards would like to forget. Yet, this crucial period between the Spanish-American War and the Spanish Civil War witnessed the birth and development of the contemporary novel in Spain.

Of the many hundreds of novels published in the first third of the twentieth century almost two hundred were written by the members of the Generation of 1898 and the Generation of 1914. All of these were taken into account when writing this book and most are mentioned, if not within the text, then in the bibliographies or in the chronology. The number analyzed at some length is on an average of twelve to fifteen novels per major author—rendering a total of nearly seventy-five works, an amount I consider large enough to be accurate as well as representative. The novels selected are in most instances the best known by each author, though at times a certain work was chosen because of its sensationalist impact (e.g., Ramón Pérez de Ayala's *A.M.D.G.*), because of its transcendence from literature to another medium (e.g., Vicente Blasco Ibáñez's several filmed versions of his novels), because of a curious absence of current scholarly attention (e.g., Ramón del Valle Inclán's trilogy of the Carlist War), or for some other distinguishing characteristic. In many cases the grouping of several works into one single category by means of varying criteria—novels with the same protagonist (e.g., Gabriel Miró's Sigüenza books), with the same theme setting (Blasco's Valencian works), with title variations (e.g., Valle's *Sonatas*), bipartite works (e.g., Ayala's last four novels), trilogies (e.g., most of Baroja's important novels)—allows a broader, more organic and extensive commentary upon a novelist's production than would have been possible on a novel-by-novel basis.

A transitional figure, Vicente Blasco Ibáñez—though three years younger than Miguel de Unamuno, the Generation of 1898's oldest member—represents the bridge that links the remnants of nineteenth-century Spanish realism with the twentieth-century novel. More than such acknowledged masters as Benito Pérez Galdós or Leopoldo Alas ("Clarín"), both of whom continued writing in the early 1900s but as unexciting anachronisms, Blasco single-handedly updated nineteenth-century fiction, ushering it into the twentieth century, and making it possible for the members of the Generation of 1898—whose contemporary he was but with whom he shared little—to disassociate themselves from fictional modes that had been clearly exhausted. To Blasco thus belongs the initial chapter of this book.

The Generation of 1898 constitutes a new chapter in Spanish literature, second in importance only to the Golden Age period (sixteenth and seventeenth centuries) of Cervantes, Lope de Vega, Tirso de Molina, Góngora, and Quevedo. The acrostic VABUMM taken from their last names' initials (Valle, Azorín, Baroja, Unamuno, Machado, and Maeztu) constitutes onomatopoeically the impression they made on the turn-of-the-century literary scene—a big bang. Fortunately, their political, social, and belletristic irreverence slowly evolved into a literary creativeness nearly unsurpassed not only in its prolific nature—their combined complete works run into the hundreds of tomes—but also in its protean quality—nearly all of them essayed every genre. Every one of them—save for Machado—wrote novels, all in a uniquely differing fashion from the rest. Unamuno, to whom chapter 2 is devoted, created the personal novel, an existentialist novel *avant le mot*. Baroja, as will be seen in chapter 3, wrote a fast-paced narrative fiction of adventure and struggle for life bordering on nihilism. Chapter 4 examines Valle Inclán's dualistic aesthetic-ethic preoccupation at either end of his literary career. However, because not all of the "ninety-eighters" who wrote novels can be called novelists—*sensu strictu*—some, such as Azorín, whose novels fall into the vague category of essayistic personal narratives, are considered in the concluding chapter 7.

Alongside Azorín in the final chapter, I have singled out Benjamín Jarnés, a member of the next generation, that of 1914, whose novels clearly reflect the philosopher and literary theorist José Ortega y Gasset's analysis of *deshumanización del arte* regarding the genre. This Generation of 1914, sometimes referred to by the acrostic MAJO

(Miró, Ayala, Jarnés, Ortega), neither as numerous nor as prolific as its forerunner, behaved less as a group than the Generation of 1898, and therefore its collective impact may have been smaller. Its members' literary significance is also individual and does not adhere so much to a generational tenet as their predecessors' contribution was initially thought to do. Both of the new generation's major figures in the field of the novel, Ramón Pérez de Ayala (chapter 5) and Gabriel Miró (chapter 6), exhibit totally different approaches in their novelistic creations. Ayala chooses an intellectualized process based on a profound knowledge of world literature, mythology, and the classics, and a keen interest in the novel's concept and structure. Miró elects an impressionist, sensual, and nearly autobiographical path to his fiction. In the end, both Ayala's and Miró's novels, as well as Jarnés's, by dint of their intellectual and aesthetic fixations to the detriment of a purely narrative interest typical of Baroja, can only appeal to a limited readership. They are novelists for elite or purist minorities willing to be constantly challenged or engaged and not merely entertained.

All in all, however, the outer limits of this book go beyond the years 1898 to 1936 announced in the title. Its true span far exceeds those thirty-eight years, since its beginnings are marked by Miguel de Unamuno's birth on 29 September 1864 and its conclusion brought about with Azorín's death on 2 March 1967—a century during which the influence of these two generations seldom failed to make itself felt on all other writers. The major figures—Unamuno, Baroja, Valle, Ayala, and Miró—are the only true classics of the peninsular Spanish novel of the twentieth century to date.

The bibliographies in this volume contain only the most notable data available and in nearly every instance they are limited to the genre of the novel. The chronology excludes all other publications; its dates are only the most significant in the writers' lives. The primary bibliography, similarly skeletal, lists first editions of major works and, as the sole exception, editions of complete works. To aid the reader in further research, published book-length bibliographies of each novelist are listed here. The bibliography of secondary sources annotates mainly book-length studies, and of these a very select few, so great is their number. The translations of all of the titles are taken from existing Twayne volumes—to which I refer all those interested in furthering their knowledge on these authors—whenever they were found to agree with my own interpretation of the works themselves; in several instances I felt compelled to render my own. (Works that have been published in English translation are referred to by their English titles throughout; untranslated works are referred to by the original Spanish titles.) Translations of passages from original texts are mostly mine as well. They are free interpretive renderings since I sought to convey an accurate meaning rather than the author's stylistic formulation.

Ricardo Landeira

University of Wyoming

Chronology

1864   29 September, Miguel de Unamuno born in Bilbao.

1866   28 October, Ramón María del Valle Inclán born in Vilanova de Arosa (Pontevedra).

1867   29 January, Vicente Blasco Ibáñez born in Valencia.

1872   28 December, Pío Baroja born in San Sebastián.

1873   8 June, José Martínez Ruiz (Azorín) born in Monóvar (Alicante).

1879   28 July, Gabriel Miró born in Alicante.

1880   9 August, Ramón Pérez de Ayala born in Oviedo.

1882   Blasco enrolls at the University of Valencia.

1883   Blasco serves as apprentice to popular novelist Manuel Fernández y González.

1888   7 October, Benjamín Jarnés born in Codo (Zaragoza). Azorín enrolls as a law student at the University of Valencia. Ayala enrolls at the Jesuit school of San Zoilo. Valle starts his law studies at Santiago de Compostela.

1890   Valle moves to Madrid. Blasco flees to Paris to avoid jail as an antimonarchist.

1891   Unamuno marries Concepción Lizárraga; obtains professorship in Salamanca; takes up permanent residence in that city. Blasco returns to Valencia; marries María Blasco. Baroja's family moves to Valencia.

1892   Valle visits Mexico for the first time.

1893   Baroja receives his degree in medicine. Miró's family moves to Ciudad Real.

1894   Blasco founds the daily *El Pueblo;* serializes *Arroz y tartana.* Baroja is appointed doctor in Cestona. Ayala completes his secondary education under the Jesuits.

1895   Valle publishes *Femeninas.* Blasco is jailed for one month on political charges. Baroja resigns his medical post.

1896 Blasco exiled to Italy; publishes *Flor de mayo*. Baroja becomes a baker and regular collaborator in *Germinal, El Liberal*, and *El País*. Azorín moves to Madrid. Miró begins his law studies at Valencia.

1897 Unamuno's first novel, *Paz en la guerra*.

1898 Spain is defeated by the United States. Blasco publishes *La barraca;* elected to the first of six terms in the Spanish Parliament. Jarnés begins his studies at the Pontifical University.

1900 Unamuno named president of the University of Salamanca. Blasco's *Entre naranjos*. Baroja's *Vidas sombrías* and *La casa de Aizgorri*.

1901 Blasco's *Sónnica la cortesana*, and Baroja's *Aventuras, inventos y mixtificaciones de Silvestre Paradox*. Azorín and Miró's first novels, *Diario de un enfermo* and *La mujer de Ojeda*, respectively. Miró marries Clemencia Maignon.

1902 Unamuno's *Amor y pedagogía*, Valle's *Sonata de otoño*, Blasco's *Cañas y barro*, and Azorín's *La voluntad*. Baroja gives up bakery; publishes *Camino de perfección*. Ayala moves to Madrid; begins graduate law studies.

1903 Valle's *Sonata de estío*, Blasco's *La catedral*, Azorín's *Antonio Azorín*, and Miro's *Hilván de escenas*. Baroja travels to Africa as a foreign correspondent; publishes *El mayorazgo de Labraz*. Ayala founds the magazine *Helios* with Juan Ramón Jiménez.

1904 Valle's *Sonata de primavera* and *Flor de santidad*, Baroja's *La lucha por la vida* trilogy; Azorín's *Las confesiones de un pequeño filósofo*, and Miró's *Del vivir*. Blasco moves to Madrid; publishes *El intruso*.

1905 Valle's *Sonata de invierno*, Blasco's *La bodega* and *La horda*, and Baroja's *La feria de los discretos*.

1906 Blasco is named Chevalier of Honor; publishes *La maja desnuda*. Baroja travels to London; publishes *Paradox, rey* and *Los últimos románticos*.

1907 Valle marries Josefina Blanco. Azorín serves first of five terms in Parliament. Ayala's father commits suicide; publishes first novel, *Tinieblas en las cumbres*.

1908 Valle's *Los cruzados de la causa*, Blasco's *Sangre y arena*, and Miró's *La novela de mi amigo* and *Nómada*. Baroja travels to Italy; publishes *La dama errante*. Azorín marries Julia Guinda. Jarnés leaves the seminary.

1909   Valle's *El resplandor de la hoguera* and *Gerifaltes de antaño*, Baroja's *La ciudad de la niebla* and *Zalacaín el aventurero*, and Miró's *La palma rota*, *El hijo santo* and *Los amores de Antón Hernando*. Blasco travels through South America; publishes *Los muertos mandan*.

1910   Baroja's *César o nada*, Miró's *Las cerezas del cementerio*, and Ayala's *A.M.D.G.* Blasco founds two colonies in Argentina. Jarnés enrolls at Zaragoza's College of Education seeking to become a teacher.

1911   Baroja's *Las inquietudes de Shanti Andía* and *El árbol de la ciencia*. Ayala studies art in Florence.

1912   Baroja buys his Vera del Bidasoa country house; death of his father; publishes *El mundo es ansí*. Miró's *Del huerto provinciano* and Ayala's *La pata de la raposa*.

1913   Baroja begins publication of *Las memorias de un hombre de acción*. Ayala marries the American Mabel Rick; publishes *Troteras y danzaderas*.

1914   Unamuno is dismissed as university president; publishes *Niebla*. Blasco's *Los Argonautas*.

1915   Azorín's *Tomás Rueda* and Miró's *El abuelo del rey*.

1916   Blasco's *Los cuatro jinetes del Apocalipsis* and Ayala's most important *Novelas poemáticas*. Jarnés marries Gregoria Bergua.

1917   Unamuno's *Abel Sánchez*, and Miró's *Libro de Sigüenza*.

1918   Blasco's *Mare Nostrum*.

1919   Blasco tours the United States; publishes *Los enemigos de la mujer*.

1920   Unamuno's *Tres novelas ejemplares y un prólogo* and Baroja's *La sensualidad pervertida*. Miró and Jarnés settle permanently in Madrid.

1921   Unamuno's *La tía Tula*, Miró's *Nuestro padre San Daniel*, and Ayala's *Belarmino y Apolonio*. Valle returns to Mexico.

1922   Blasco's *La tierra de todos* and *El paraíso de las mujeres*, Baroja's *La leyenda de Jaun de Alzate*, Azorín's *Don Juan*, and Miró's *Niño y grande*. Ayala receives the "Mariano de Cavia" prize.

1923   Blasco's *La reina Calafia*, Baroja's *El laberinto de las sirenas*, and Ayala's *Luna de miel, Luna de hiel*, and *Los trabajos de Urbano y Simona*. Miguel Primo de Rivera stages his successful coup d'etat.

1924 Unamuno is exiled by Primo de Rivera. Baroja's *La figuras de cera*. Azorín is elected to the Spanish Royal Academy.

1925 Blasco remarries after death of his first wife; publishes *El papa del mar*. Baroja's *La nave de los locos* and Azorín's *Doña Inés*. Miró is awarded "Mariano de Cavia" prize.

1926 Valle's *Tirano Banderas*, Blasco's *A los pies de Venus*, Baroja's *El gran torbellino del mundo* and *Las veleidades de la fortuna*, Miró's *El obispo leproso*, Ayala's *Tigre Juan* and *El curandero de su honra*, and Jarnés's *El profesor inútil*.

1927 Unamuno's Spanish version of *Cómo se hace una novela*, Valle's *La corte de los milagros*, and Baroja's *Los amores tardíos*.

1928 Valle's *Viva mi dueño*, Azorín's *El caballero inactual*, Miró's *Años y leguas*, Ayala's *Justicia*, and Jarnés's *El convidado de papel*. 28 January, Blasco dies in France. Ayala is elected to the Spanish Royal Academy.

1929 Blasco's posthumous *En busca del Gran Kan* and *El caballero de la Virgen*, Baroja's *Los pilotos de altura*, Azorín's *Pueblo*, and Jarnés's *Locura y muerte de nadie* and *Paula y Paulita*.

1930 Baroja's *La estrella del Capitán Chimista* and Jarnés's *Teoría del zumbel* and *Viviana y Merlín*. Primo de Rivera's dictatorship ends. 27 May, Miró dies.

1931 King Alfonso XIII is forced to leave Spain. The Second Spanish Republic is proclaimed. Ayala begins his term as ambassador to Great Britain. Jarnés's *Escenas junto a la muerte*.

1932 Valle's *Baza de espadas* begins serialization in *El sol;* divorces his wife; his publisher files for bankruptcy. Baroja's trilogy *La selva oscura*.

1933 Unamuno's *San Manuel Bueno, mártir y tres historias más* and Jarnés's *Fauna contemporánea*. Valle is appointed director of the Spanish Academy of Fine Arts in Rome.

1934 Unamuno retires as professor; wife dies. Baroja is elected as member of the Spanish Royal Academy; publishes *Las noches del Buen Retiro*.

1936 6 January, Valle dies. 18 July, Civil War begins. Baroja, Azorín, and Ayala flee to Paris. Baroja's *El cura de Monleón* and Jarnés's *Don Alvaro o la fuerza del tino*. 31 December, Unamuno dies.

1939   1 April, Civil War ends. Baroja, Azorín, and Ayala return to Spain. Jarnés goes to Mexico in exile.

1940   Jarnés's *La novia del viento*. Ayala takes up residence in Buenos Aires until 1954.

1942   Azorín's *El escritor*.

1943   Baroja's *El caballero de Erlaiz*, Azorín's *El enfermo* and *Capricho*, and Jarnés's *Venus dinámica*.

1944   Azorín's *La isla sin aurora*, *María Fontán*, and *Salvadora de Olbena* and Jarnés's *Constelación de Friné*.

1948   Jarnés returns to Spain; publishes *Eufrosina o la gracia*.

1949   Ayala travels to France and Spain. 10 August, Jarnés dies in Madrid.

1952   Baroja's *Las veladas del Chalet Gris*.

1953   Baroja's *Los amores de Antonio y Cristina*.

1956   30 October, Baroja dies in Madrid.

1957   Ayala's *Obras selectas*.

1962   5 August, Ayala dies in Madrid.

1967   2 March, Azorín dies in Madrid.

Chapter One
Vicente Blasco Ibáñez: The Naturalist Novel

By the early 1880s realism had run its course not only in Europe but also in Spain. The writings of the French novelist Emile Zola (1840–1902) and the commotion brought about by his publication of *Thérèse Raquin* (1867), along with other novels that typify the brutality, fatalism, and scatology of naturalism, dealt a death blow to realism's long-lived preeminence in European literature. Such works ensured that Zola and the theories and techniques of naturalism were at the heart of most literary polemics throughout Europe. Few people in Spain had heard of the French writer prior to 1877 and even fewer had read any of his books, but in the wake of *L'Assomoir* (*The Dram-Shop,* 1877), *naturalism* became a literary buzzword in Spanish newspapers and magazines.[1] Although one of his short stories ("The Attack of the Windmill") had been translated into Spanish in 1879, it was not until one year later that the novels *The Dram-Shop, Nana* (1880), and *Une Page d'Amour* (A page of love) were made available to Spanish readers. They met with unqualified success, if one may judge by the three translations done of both *Nana* and *The Dram-Shop* within one year of their Spanish publication. Establishment critics in Spain were not enthusiastic over this irreverent and often obscene fiction, but Zola found unstinting support among the younger writers. His true apologist, the one who most vigorously defended him, was the Countess Emilia Pardo Bazán (1851–1921), herself a budding novelist who by 1883, the date of publication of her book on naturalism titled *La cuestión palpitante* (The burning question), had written no fewer than six books, both fiction and criticism.

Naturalism in Spain

In the preface of her early novel, *Un viaje de novios* (A honeymoon, 1881), Pardo Bazán began her campaign in favor of the new French

1

school, essaying some naturalistic techniques in the work itself.[2] It was not until 1883 that she devoted herself in earnest to Zola's theories in a series of newspaper articles in Madrid's *La Epoca* that were later collected into a volume, the above-mentioned *La cuestión palpitante*. The slim tome was prefaced by Leopoldo Alas "Clarín" (1852–1901), author of the single most perfect example of the nineteenth-century Spanish novel, *La Regenta* (The regent's wife, 1884). In these essays, Pardo Bazán produced a perceptive and well-reasoned critique of naturalism. To be sure, *La cuestión palpitante* gave rise to numerous attacks not only upon Zola and naturalism but also upon Pardo Bazán and her "advanced" ideas.

Emile Zola's brand of naturalism was a pseudoscientific approach to literature, specifically the novel, wherein direct observation substituted for creative imagination. Philosophically it drew a great deal on August Comte's (1798–1857) positivistic theories and Adolphe Taine's (1828–93) deterministic ideology. Zola derived naturalism's objectivist and imitative tenets from the methodology of experimental medicine advanced by the physician Claude Bernard (1813–78). Psychopathological and undesirable behavior patterns such as incest, alcoholism, and other depravities, which Zola and his school took to be lower social-class phenomena, anchored naturalist narrative fiction in the guise of documented treatises. Gone were man's ideals, spiritual dimensions, and optimism. These, together with the novelist's right to a lyrical style, were displaced by base instinct, materialism, determinism, and behavioristic, coarse, and minute descriptions. In Zola's conception of the new novelistic mode, instruction, not diversion, was the goal. The typical scenario of the naturalist novel, then, pits characters devoid of spiritual convictions, poor, uneducated, burdened with numerous children, cursed with alcoholism or other debilitating illnesses (tuberculosis was another favorite) against the indifference of nature (or society), putting beyond their reach the means by which to overcome their plight or the serenity necessary to cope with their lot.

Such base and redemptionless principles ran counter to the religious beliefs held by most Spaniards living in the latter part of the nineteenth century. Even the usual liberal intellectual groups, including many writers, found such crude and fatalistic thinking unpalatable. Complete denial of a spiritual dimension in man was for them simply unacceptable. Thus, naturalism in crossing the border into Spain underwent a radical amputation and became a technique without an ideology—no Spanish novelist had the stomach for the strong stuff that made up Zola's godless and pessimistic determinism. But, if on the one hand the ultimate damning of man is hard to find in the Spanish novel of this period, on the other hand, themes, characters, settings, descriptions, and techniques bearing Zola's undeniable stamp of the sordid and the materialistic, by their profligacy, attest to the deep and lasting influence of French naturalism in the writings of not only Pardo Bazán, but on those of Leopoldo Alas "Clarín," Benito Pérez Galdós (1843–1920), Armando Palacio Valdés (1853–1938), José María de Pereda (1833–1906), and Vicente Blasco Ibáñez (1867–1928). Such elements extend well into the twentieth century in the works of Felipe Trigo (1865–1916) and Emilio Carrere (1880–1947), in Azorín's (1873–1967) *La Voluntad* (Willpower) written in 1902, and in two early novels of Ramón Pérez de Ayala (1881–1962), *Tinieblas en las cumbres* (Darkness on the heights) and *Troteras y danzaderas* (Mummers and dancers) dating from 1907 and 1913 respectively. Thus, none of the best of the turn-of-the-century novelists escaped naturalism's spell.

Naturalism, then, lasted in Spain from the 1880s[3] until its waning in the 1920s as a recognizable force, though it survives as an identifiable trait to this date in such writers as Camilo José Cela (1916–). It coexisted with the Generation of 1898, antedating it by a few years much as does its greatest practitioner in the Spanish novel, Vincente Blasco Ibáñez. Blasco should have belonged to this famous group of "ninety-eighters" by age and ideology, though his literary bent and political activism differ from theirs, as does his temperament for being a man of action, not contenting himself as Miguel de Unamuno (1864–1936) and others did with merely writing and speaking about reform. Blasco is the most visible bridge between the nineteenth and twentieth century in Spanish letters because, while never throwing aside the fundamental rules of Zola's naturalism, he produced a fiction that at the same time was popular, innovative, diverse, and of lasting interest.

The Picturesque Life of Vicente Blasco Ibáñez

Vicente Blasco Ibáñez was born in the Mediterranean coastal city of Valencia on 29 January, 1867. His parents, Gaspar Blasco Teruel and Ramona Ibáñez Martínez, a prosperous middle-class Aragonese couple, first sent him to a religious convent where the young Vicente lasted only a few months, being expelled for his censurable behavior in the school's chapel. This incident of rebelliousness marks the beginning of a chronicled biography that reads like an adventure story worthy of Blasco the novelist. Pranks such as the one that caused his expulsion from elementary school made Vicente popular with his classmates, though other pursuits endeared him equally with his superiors, activities that early on pointed to his future as a writer. The most notable of these, begun while still in grade school, consisted of writing a newspaper made up of several stapled pages filled with short stories and brief news items. This news sheet was circulated among his young friends and celebrated by those fortunate enough to get a chance to read it.

As a high school student Blasco showed no better than average diligence, preferring to wander the streets of his hometown rather than to sit in a classroom, and to consume books on travel and adventure instead of those texts assigned by his teachers. A lack of interest in formal studies prompted him to devote his time to doing what he liked best—writing for publication. He began collaborating in a small local weekly of known liberal leanings, *El Turia* (named after Valencia's river), which further stirred in him a desire to take part in the city's political intrigues of the day. When Blasco entered the University of Valencia to study law at the age of fifteen he already had a minor reputation as both a writer and a revolutionary. Behind him were several published short stories, the first of which, "La torre de Boatella" (The tower of Boatella), had been written in the Valencian dialect,[4] and one novel titled *Carmen* on whose back cover the enterprising author advertised forthcoming volumes.[5] At the university Blasco continued to follow his habit of absenteeism from classes, choosing instead to maintain a largely bohemian existence of frequenting political meetings and producing commentaries and stories for newspapers. Aided by a prodigious photographic memory, he would busy himself with the course texts a few weeks prior to final examinations, a system that never seems to have failed him.

No longer satisfied with a schedule that most young men would find overwhelming, Blasco ran away to Madrid on 8 December, 1883, leaving a farewell letter to his parents informing them he was leaving for Barcelona—a ruse that worked for a time. In Madrid,

living in a fleabag boardinghouse and doing without more than just
a few meals, he met with constant failure. Unable to secure a position
as a reporter in any republican (i.e., liberal) newspaper, he chanced
upon the position of secretary-amanuensis to Manuel Fernández y
González (1821–88), the old and now sickly purveyor of romantic
potboilers. During his brief stint as Fernández's aide, more often
than not, Blasco (finding that the old man had fallen asleep while
dictating) would finish the installment novels himself. When on 2
February, 1884 his father's friend, the newsman Peris Mencheta,
ran into Blasco at a political rally, the young man was dragged back
to Valencia, thus ending his alliance with the old and impecunious
Fernández, and just in time, as it turned out, for him to participate
in that year's student riots at the university. Though during his
early years Blasco despised literary gatherings, thinking them effete
circles, and being drawn instead to heated political meetings, he
liked very much to listen to classical music. As often as he found
the time, he attended opera performances and symphony concerts.
Blasco's idols in this curious passion were Wagner and Beethoven,
whose marble busts were placed alongside those of Cervantes and
Victor Hugo, his literary heroes, in his various homes.

By the time he had graduated from law school in 1888, Blasco's
literary undertakings were considerable. On a regular basis he wrote
for the paper *El Correo Valenciano* where among his best stories to
date were : "Fantasías" (Fantasies), "El Conde Garci-Fernández"
(Count Garci-Fernández), "Romeu el Guerrillero" (Romeu the guer-
rilla fighter), "El adiós de Schubert" (Schubert's farewell), "Made-
moiselle Norma" (Miss Norma), and "Caerse del cielo" (To fall from
heaven). Madrid magazines and other regional newspapers were also
likely to carry pieces by Blasco on any given day. On a par with
his belletristic prowess was his political activism, intended always
to further a liberal cause. A fiery speech of his in late December
1889 aroused too many antimonarchical sentiments among a sizable
crowd to go unnoticed by the police, and Blasco was sought for
days by state authorities determined to throw the agitator in jail.
He fled the country, crossing the border into France where he settled
in Paris for almost two years. His return to Spain was carried out
under an 1891 amnesty decree handed down by the government.

In November of the year of his return to Valencia, Blasco married
his first cousin, María Blasco del Cacho. This change of civil status,
however, did not translate into an ideological or political mellowing

for him. On the contrary, his pen became almost exclusively a political weapon. The volumes *Historia de la revolución española, 1808– 1874* (History of the spanish revolution), *¡Viva la República!* (Long live the republic!), *Los fanáticos* (The fanatics), *La araña negra* (The black spider), and *El juez* (The judge), published between 1892 and 1894, all excoriate the monarchy, its supporters, and the ultraconservative Catholic church and its ideologies. The last title belongs to a drama that enjoyed some public acclaim. Blasco, unfortunately unable to savor this success due to the death of his mother on the night of the premiere, never wrote another line for the theater. More and more his interests seemed to be wholly political, taking over the sphere of earlier purely fictional writings. He opened a publishing house called "La Propaganda Democrática" where the first book issued was a translation, done by Blasco himself, of several of Voltaire's works and featuring a prologue by no less a figure than Victor Hugo. As if this political arm were not enough, perhaps because he felt the need for a more direct voice, Blasco poured every cent he had into the founding of a morning newspaper, *El Pueblo,* which began publication on 12 November, 1894. This daily, written almost single-handedly by Blasco, also carried short stories by Emile Zola and Guy de Maupassant (1850–93) as well as serialized versions of his own first five novels. The most immediate results derived from this new venture were the long hours that Blasco had to spend writing, composing, editing, and advertising the paper, and the mounting fines that nearly each edition garnered from the municipal authorities. On almost all counts, *El Pueblo* repeatedly bordered on extinction in its period of infancy. Finally Blasco went too far when toward the end of 1895 he endorsed the plan of Francisco Pi y Margall (president of the first Spanish Republic who lived from 1824 to 1901) to grant political autonomy to the insurgents of the Spanish colony of Cuba. In *El Pueblo* universal conscription for military service, freedom of speech, political assembly, and numerous other libertarian causes were stridently advocated, leading to riots and police barricades in the streets of Valencia. As a result Blasco had to go into hiding and flee Spain for the second time in four years. Once again he went to France but did not stay there, proceeding to Italy where he lived in Genoa. As he had done in Paris (producing the collection of essays *París, impresiones de un emigrado* [Paris, impressions of an exile] in 1893), in Italy Blasco wrote the travel sketches *En el país del arte (In the Land of Art)* in 1896, which first appeared in *El Pueblo*.

Upon his return to Spain Blasco was sentenced to several years in prison and actually served over twelve months of incarceration. According to his own count, this was but one of over thirty jail sentences he received for political reasons during his lifetime. His release from prison (after the sentence was commuted through influential political and family friends) moved Blasco to run for the office of congressional representative from Valencia for the national legislature (the Spanish *Cortes*). If elected, this office would give him political immunity from the type of offense he had so often been charged with. Blasco not only succeeded in being elected to six consecutive terms, but in the end he bowed out, having grown tired of the post after constituting his own party of political followers—the Blasquistas.

Famous and rich from the earnings of his books, Blasco built an ostentatious neo-Greek mansion, complete with marble columns, called "La Malvarrosa" (The Pink Hollyhock"), where he welcomed other writers and students of literature. He made trips to South America as a guest of heads of state, toured Argentina where he founded two cities that he named Cervantes and Nueva Valencia, and for six years stopped writing novels altogether, devoting himself to lecturing, traveling, and exploring parts of the world he had not seen before. He returned to France at the beginning of World War I and in Paris wrote what was to become his most celebrated work, *Los cuatro jinetes del Apocalipsis (The Four Horsemen of the Apocalypse)*, in support of the Allied cause in 1916. His fame seemed to grow with each of his books, several of which were made into Hollywood films, and foreign governments conferred honors and decorations upon him. He came to the United States in October 1919 and remained in this country until the following July. During those months he was received into the U.S. House of Representatives, was presented with an honorary doctorate from George Washington University, and made an extensive lecture tour throughout the eastern United States.

In his late fifties Blasco's work began to slowly lose its vigor and literary worth, yet he could not bring himself to stop writing even when supposedly resting. When on 23 October, 1923 he embarked on a six-month cruise around the world, the end result, as usual, was a book, a three-volume work appropriately titled *La vuelta al mundo de un novelista (A Novelist's Tour of the World).* Immensely wealthy from his writings and film rights, and once again at odds with the Spanish government, Blasco bought a large estate in Menton, on the French Riviera, where he lived the last years of his life. He died there on 28 January, 1928, one day before his sixty-first birthday, as he worked on a sequel to be called "The Fifth Horseman of the Apocalypse." His second wife, the Chilean aristocrat Elena Ortúzar Bulnes, survived him for many years, dying in the mid-sixties.

The Art of Blasco Ibáñez

Although by 1898 he was widely known and more famous than any other living Spanish author, save perhaps for the popular Benito Pérez Galdós whose star had begun to wane, Blasco's best work was still to come as were those later novels that would extend his fame across the world and make him wealthy. Blasco boasted of being the least literary of writers,[6] considering himself a man of action who wrote impelled by an unshakable need. He combined the stamina of the first with the *furor poeticus* of the second to produce an astonishing volume of prose—over one hundred tomes have been published, not including Blasco's thousands of pages written in newspapers and magazines. Of those hundred-odd volumes, some thirty are novels. In a letter written in 1918 to his friend Julio Cejador y Frauca (1864–1927), a major critic of the time and author of the fourteen-volume *Historia de la lengua y literatura castellanas* (A history of the Castillian language and literature, 1915–20), Blasco wrote: "I carry a novel (sometimes two or three) in my head for a long time, but when the moment to externalize it arrives I work feverishly, I live an existence that you might call subconscious, and I write the book in the amount of time that it would take an amanuensis simply to copy it."[7] Writing at a ten-hour pace each day, Blasco normally managed to finish one of his novels in approximately three months.

He was a great narrator and expository writer, and such a masterful literary painter of landscapes that he has been compared often with his friend the Valencian impressionist artist Joaquín Sorolla (1863–1923). Blasco's descriptive passages of his native region, the faithfully reproduced dialogues of local speech in their idiomatic nuances, make for vivid and powerful stories set in exuberant backdrops where no levity or relief of any sort exists to soften a world of powerful instincts, sensations, and violence. Inextricably lost in these primeval scenarios are Blasco's characters, pitiable creatures whose physiological traits operate in detriment of an already atrophied spiritual dimension—such is the imprint of Zola's influence. And yet the weight of Maupassant, Flaubert (1821–80), and Anatole France (1844–1924) cannot be wholly dismissed, for they too left an impression on the young Blasco, as a reader, which later surfaced in his careful crafting of narrative structures and in his unforgettable gallery of individualized personages.

In the same letter to Cejador cited earlier, Blasco classified his novelistic output into the following divisions: regional novels, thesis novels, psychological novels, cosmopolitan novels, historical novels, American novels, and novels of adventure. Most of them have a true biographical ring, especially his Valencian or regional novels. The settings of the Albufera and the Huerta, as well as many secondary characters such as Copa, Pimentó, Cañamel, Morte, and even some of the buildings described, down to Barret's shack, really existed and were recognizable to people in the area.[8] Blasco himself lived through many of the adventures unfolded in his books of fiction.

The Regional Novels

Blasco's "Valencian novels" are disturbing tales of elementary passions (greed, lust, hate), of primitive forces (hunger, poverty, sickness, fear, death), and of the overpowering dominance of nature, at once beautiful and awesome, a threatening and all-controlling background against which characters are dwarfed or altogether disappear. All of these novels have a foreshadowed end from the very outset, an inevitability that is tragic in a classical sense—though a flaw damages the characters both from within (classical hero) and from without (romantic hero); they are doomed by their own deeds but also by an indifferent and, at times, malevolent environment (e.g., nature, fate, society). Blasco has stacked the deck against them in a throwback to the naturalist aesthetic. The settings are full-color portrayals of true Valencian land- and seascapes, exaggerated and stylized to conform to the milieu of the story at hand. At times they are violent, at others subdued. Sometimes they threaten and, though peaceful at given intervals, they are always disquieting.

The spectrum is wide because context often requires it, but the fundamental fidelity with which it is reproduced remains constant.

The novels that most endear Blasco to the critics and assure his place among the best fiction writers of the turn of the century are those he wrote first, these so-called regional novels. They are *Arroz y tartana (The Three Roses,* 1894), *Flor de mayo (The Mayflower,* 1896), *La barraca (The Cabin,* 1898), *Entre naranjos (The Torrent,* 1900), and *Cañas y barro (Reeds and Mud,* 1902). Two books of short stories, *Cuentos valencianos* (Valencian tales, 1896), and *La condenada* (The condemned woman, 1900), plus a period novel, *Sónnica la cortesana (Sonnica the Courtesan,* 1901), set in the Valencia of the Carthaginean conquest (219 B.C.), complete Blasco's regional cycle. Among these, undisputably his best works and perhaps the only novels recognizable as uniquely Blasco's, three tower above the rest: *The Three Roses, The Cabin,* and *Reeds and Mud.* They alone possess a permanent human and literary worth.

The Mayflower depicts the toils and misery of a small town's waterfront inhabitants, the fishermen and their families. In sharper focus, it views the lives of two brothers of opposite character, Pascual and Tonet, who end up dying (fratricide and suicide) as a result of envy and marital infidelity. Brutal in its drama and emotions, *The Mayflower* (named after Pascual's boat) falls squarely in the Zolaesque mold of dark and pessimistic naturalism. *The Torrent,* set in the midst of a fragrant citrus orchard, stands as Blasco's most passionate love story. Here Rafael Brull, the rich scion of a politically influential family, falls in love with an opera diva, Leonora Brunna, only to see the relationship spoiled by his authoritarian mother, Ramona. When Rafael later attempts to win back Leonora, she spurns him for his lack of resolve. In *The Torrent,* the impact of naturalism is lessened by the love sentiment and the sensual synesthesia of the orange grove setting, though the factors of heredity and environment result in an expected determinism. The Greta Garbo film of *The Torrent,* adapted liberally from the novel, was the first of many motion pictures derived from Blasco's works. *Sonnica the Courtesan,* also set in Valencia along with *El papa del mar (The Pope of the Sea,* 1925), and some three others, belongs to the realm of the historical novels because of its chronologically removed plot—the siege of the city of Sagunto by Hannibal in the year 219 B.C. This heroic chapter in the history of the Valencian city caught up in the Second Punic War between Carthage and Rome (ending in the mass suicide of its inhabitants who refused to surrender after being encircled for nine months) owes less to any literary aesthetic than to a novelistic vogue of the times. Flaubert's *Salammbô*, (1862), Pierre Louÿ's (1870–1925) *Aphrodite* (1896), and Henryk Sienkienwicz's (1846–1916) *Quo Vadis?* (1896) are but a sample of the archaeological-historical novels being written at the time Blasco published his *Sonnica the Courtesan,* though he claimed that his had been inspired by an obscure verse composition belonging to the Sevillian poet Silio Itálico (25–100 A.D.).[9]

The Three Roses, the first of Blasco's regional novels, remains, in spite of the many to follow it, one of his masterpieces. It is thoroughly naturalistic in its choice of characters (petite bourgeousie), themes (poverty, degradation, envy), and tone (pessimism and impending doom). Setting the story in the almost contemporary Valencia of the late 1800s, Blasco narrates the miserable existence of a lower middle-class family, the Pajares, which, impelled by the wife Manuela's desire to emulate the richer Valencianos, comes to a shameful end through financial ruin and death. Taking his cue and title from the popular air "Arrós y tartana, / y rode la bola / a la valençiana" ("Rice and a carriage, / and let the ball bounce / in a carefree fashion"). Blasco rails mercilessly against the petite bourgeoisie who, like Manuela, live for today beyond their means, not caring for tomorrow's consequences or for those who will ultimately suffer for it all. In the case of the Pajares clan, the villain is Doña Manuela who deliberately chose not to marry for love the first time around, doing it instead for money, only to have her former lover and second husband later spend all of her inheritance and plunge the family into monumental debt. When even her son Juanito is compelled to have his girlfriend gamble with her life savings in order to provide funds for Doña Manuela's extravagances, the reader truly begins to gauge her insane profligacy. And yet not content with everyone's economic ruin, the self-centered Doña Manuela sinks further into her own moral degradation by prostituting herself to a shopkeeper in order to obtain money with which to buy another carriage horse to replace their dead one, thus avoiding the necessity of strolling through the Valencia boulevards on the weekends, and instead, riding like the moneyed aristocrats. Sadly enough, the death of the carriage horse represents the climax of *The Three Roses,* symbolizing emptiness and lack of meaning in an existence of ostentation, pretentiousness, and envy. On the other hand, the deaths of the young Juanito and of the old Don Eugenio, both succumbing indirectly as a result of Doña Manuela's impecunious taste for the good life, are hardly essential to the development of the narrative. As in most naturalistic novels, there are only victims; *The Three Roses* is a profoundly deterministic work in which egoism, greed, and hate triumph at the end. Only the beautiful *costumbrista* (local color) scenes depicting the 19 March celebration of the Valencia *fallas* (fireworks celebration on St. Joseph's day), Christmas time, the St. Vincent patron-day feast, the holy processions of Corpus Christi, and other pagan (bullfights) as well as Christian holidays offer the reader a mild relief from Blasco's depressing Zolaesque catalog of human wretchedness.

Together with the birth of the poet and playwright Federico García Lorca (1898–1936), the single most important event for Spanish letters in 1898 was the publication of *The Cabin*. This novel, which conferred upon Blasco international renown, almost did not succeed in being published. Its genesis, as the author recalls it in a later (1925) prologue, constitutes a fascinating narrative in itself. The events that led to Blasco's having to flee Valencia around the middle of 1895, it will be remembered, were a result of his active part in demonstrations seeking independence for Spain's American colonies. While hiding in the attic of a tavern owned by a republican youth and his mother, in wait for a ship that was to take him to Italy, Blasco read several books but soon grew tired of inactivity and asked for writing paraphernalia. Provided with pen, ink, and three small notebooks, he wrote a short story titled "Venganza moruna" (Moorish revenge) in two afternoons. When the night of his departure came, in the rush to get away, Blasco left everything including the notebooks completely filled with writing on both sides of the pages. Almost two years later at a political rally, Blasco, by then an elected representative, recognized the young man who had given him refuge in his house. The two returned to the tavern where the faded pages of "Venganza moruna" together with everything else forgotten were given back to their owner. Rather than publishing it in its original form—his confessed first inclination—Blasco decided to expand it into a full-length novel.

Since in those days his newspaper, *El Pueblo*, took up most of Blasco's time, work on the future novel was truly a labor of love. "I have never worked while so physically tired nor with such a concentrated and determined enthusiasm," he subsequently declared.[10] From two o'clock until five in the morning Blasco wrote as in a frenzy until the ten chapters were finished, changing the title to *The Cabin* and saving the earlier one of "Venganza moruna" for another story. He serialized *The Cabin,* as he had done with previous novels, in *El Pueblo,* but apparently few readers took notice of it. Its second showing, in book form, was equally inauspicious. Published by his friend Federico Sempere in an edition of seven hundred copies, *The Cabin* sold no more than five hundred copies, most of them in and around Valencia. The total profit came to seventy-eight pesetas, which had to be split between author and publisher. These meager proceeds might have sealed the novel's future if Professor Hérelle from the Lyceum in Bayonne had not picked up the book at the San Sebastián railroad station while waiting for his train back to France. So impressed was Hérelle with *The Cabin* that he wrote several unanswered letters to its author asking permission to translate it into French, and Blasco eventually gave his consent. It was many months later when reading his morning paper in Madrid that Blasco found that *La Cabane,* as it was called in France, had met with not only critical but popular success in Paris. As a result, *El Liberal* (which subsequently serialized it) and other Madrid dailies echoed the French press's enthusiasm for the novel, causing sales to soar in Spain. *The Cabin,* between its 1898 introduction and the cited 1925 prologue, had sold over one million copies worldwide. It was perhaps the first time a Spanish author had enjoyed such a best-seller in his lifetime.

   The Cabin is a relentless and cruel rendering of the lives of the laborer Batiste, his wife, and four children as they strive tirelessly to survive in the fields deserted by Tío Barret—a plot of farmland accursed by the murder of its usurious owner Don Salvador at the hands of the former tenant Barret. The straightforward narrative (its simplicity due in part to its origins as a short story) depicts the unrewarding struggle of Batiste and his family to overcome the arduous labors of working the soil and rebuilding their cabin, in addition to facing the prejudices and enmity of the neighboring villagers. The local warden, Pimentó, embodies the hatred of the local inhabitants as his actions victimize every member of the struggling family. Their irrigation rights are taken away on trumped-up charges, the daughter Roseta's romance is broken up, five-year-old Pascualet dies as a result of being pushed into an infested stream, their plow horse is stabbed to death, Batiste is shot in the back, and finally the cabin is set on fire together with all of the grain from their first harvest.

Set in the real village of Alboraya, *The Cabin* is devastating in its portrayal of injustice, man's inhumanity to man, and human powerlessness to overcome obstacles that life presents as a matter of course, either as a consequence of the evil character of others or as a result of nature's own indifference to humanity's plight. Murder, robbery, and deceit on one side and drought, fire, and hard labor on the other, conspire in the inevitable doom that preys on Batiste and his brood. Try as they might, they can do nothing to change the outcome that fate reserves for them.

With the publication of *Reeds and Mud* in 1902 the regional cycle is brought to a close. This novel was justly regarded by Blasco as his most solid and accomplished work.[11] It represents not only the best among the Valencian novels but also the one on which most critics lavish their praise. *Reeds and Mud* epitomizes Zola's naturalism blended with Blasco's own regional *costumbrismo,* the power of which is sufficiently enduring to arrest even today's reader. The brutality and determinism of the earlier regional works persist in this one, but in addition there appears a stylization of color and landscape bordering on the poetic. The changing settings of the Albufera with its island village of El Palomar, its marshes of La Dehesa, and its impenetrable forests—all in different seasons and at different hours of the day—have no equal in Spanish literature. The plot of *Reeds and Mud* is more diverse than that of *The Cabin,* but fundamentally its tenets are the same: man's struggle against his own nature, against other men, and against the circumstances that surround him. The setting has not changed much either: a village of thatched-roof huts built of "reeds and mud." And neither have the characters who personify manifold evils: adultery, gluttony, indolence, murder, poverty, and usury. The strongest forces of sex, instinct, and a sinister nature once again prevail over the main characters in a foreseeable ruination. In *Reeds and Mud* Tío Toni cultivates his rice fields while the son Tonet whiles away time flirting with Neleta, wife of the rich and sickly bar owner Cañamel. Fortune smiles upon the lazy and shameless Tonet who becomes Cañamel's business partner, availing himself not only of his wines and food but of his wife as well. Formerly childhood sweethearts, Tonet and Neleta, even after Cañamel's death (from obesity, alcoholism, and idleness), cannot marry, forbidden by the dead man's will, which stipulates she must remain single in order to inherit his wealth. Furtively attracted by lust, but legally kept apart by greed, Neleta and Tonet continue their covert affair from which a child is born. A victim of his own weaknesses, Tonet agrees to Neleta's order to drown his own son, but later shoots himself in remorse. In this ambience of marsh fever, of slimy eels, of reeds and mud, lust displaces love, blind ambition becomes greed, and malice darkens every sentiment. In *Reeds and Mud* the characters, in spite of an individuality underscored by baseness, pale beside the awesome nature which surrounds, oppresses, and ultimately destroys them. The import of their flaws only serves to accelerate their tragic ends. Again in this case, nothing and no one—least of all themselves—can stave off final destruction.

The Doctrinal, Psychological, Cosmopolitan, Historical, and American Novels

Following the regional novel cycle, Blasco undertook the writing of another series, which he labeled "thesis novels." These four works show the author's social, religious, and political ideals, to the detriment of their fictionalized content. All carry an explicit message that damages to a large extent the illusion of a self-contained narrative microcosm. The characters seem to be no more than flat icons, motivated principally by concerns of reform or progress. In *La catedral* (*The Shadow of the Cathedral*, 1903), Blasco's anticlerical bent offers up a story of the revolutionary Gabriel Luna who dies a failed man while trying to safeguard the jewels of the Virgin in the Cathedral of Toledo. *El intruso* (*The Intruder*, 1904), also in a religious vein, comments on the power of the Society of Jesus over the Catholic church in Spain, particularly in the Basque region where its action takes place. *La horda* (*The Mob*, 1905) has as the main theme social inequality and as its protagonist a cynical Madrid newspaper reporter, Isidro Maltrana, hardened by constant exposure to the city's lower classes and criminal elements. *La bodega* (*The Fruit of the Vine*, 1905), set in the southern city of Jerez de la Frontera, famous for its sherry wines, rails against the ills of drinking. It also analyzes the political and social conditions in the Andalusian region, which—in view of Blasco's socialist ideology—warrant all of the anarchist propaganda spread by the agitator Fernando Salvatierra against the prosperous landowners and vintners. The four novels represent, at best, the subgenre sometimes called engagé literature, wherein its author artistically (i.e., implicitly) shows a commitment to a cause he feels worthwhile and which does not detract from novelistic plot, characters, style, themes, or structure. At their worst, *The Shadow of the Cathedral* and remaining thesis novels come across as a propagandist's doctrinal ax-grinding. Often, it seems, Blasco forgot that a novel may contain sociology, philosophy, history, or any other discipline insofar as it does not become so saturated with them that it then turns out to be a sociological, philosophical, or historical treatise and stops being an autonomous piece of fiction.[12]

The next series, appropriately "psychological novels," offers character studies. In them Blasco placed his protagonists in chosen ambients and then developed and observed their existence. There are usually thought to be five works in this cycle. *La maja desnuda* (*Woman Triumphant,* 1906), titled after Goya's masterpiece canvas, narrates the life of the famous painter Mariano Renovales, the undoing of his wife resulting from his marital infidelity, and Mariano's own death from remorse. *La voluntad de vivir* (The will to live), though written and abortively published in 1907, was not issued in a second edition until 1953, two years after the death of its heroine since, fashioned as a roman à clef, Blasco felt that both of its protagonists, if identified, could suffer needlessly. The entire first edition (12,000 copies) was destroyed in Valencia at Blasco's expense and behest. *La voluntad de vivir* recounts the passionate love affair between an older man, Dr. Enrique Valdivia (patterned after a well-known Madrid University professor), and Lucha (modeled after a foreign siren), a young Valenzuelan girl. Lucha's promiscuity and Enrique's violent jealousy lead to his suicide and her final repentance. *Sangre y arena* (*The Blood of the Arena,* 1908), often derided as a mere portrayal of the "typical" Spain depicted in bullfight and tourist travel posters, really comes across as the best example of an admittedly none-too-laudable subgenre. It recounts the rise and fall of the fortunes of the bullfighter Juan Gallardo (modeled after Antonio Fuentes) who, though wealthy and married, aspires to the love of the aristocrat Doña Sol. Against a well-documented backdrop of the art of tauromachy, Blasco portrays the struggles of Gallardo as he tries to win the favors of Doña Sol and the applause of the crowd, a double quest that brings about his death when he is gored by his final bull of the afternoon.

The title *Los muertos mandan* (*The Dead Command,* 1909), reveals the theme of this novel, in which a young and penniless nobleman is prohibited by the traditions and beliefs of his dead ancestors from seeking love and happiness in a life of his own. Conceived as a two-volume work, this novel, set in the Balearic isles of Mallorca and Ibiza, explores the theme of interfaith marriage between a Catholic and a Jew with the triumph of personal choice over established, outmoded, and prejudiced norms. *Luna Benamor* (1909), a *nouvelle* whose title derives from the name of its female protagonist, plumbs once more the question of marriage between people of different faiths. Here, the Spanish diplomat Luis Aguirre falls in love in the city of Gibraltar with the granddaughter of a rich Sephardic Jewish banker. While Aguirre succeeds in making Luna fall in love with him, the grandfather Aboab and the rest of the family refuse to give their permission for the wedding. In these five novels Blasco pitted his protagonists against the odds that their circumstances repre-sented. In only one, *The Dead Command,* did the hero Jaime Febrer triumph over his dilemma, forcing his will (search for love and happiness) to triumph over adversity (poverty, tradition, and an-cestral obligation). In *Woman Triumphant,* the painter Mariano Re-novales succumbs to adultery and causes the death of his wife as well as his own. In *La voluntad de vivir,* Enrique Valdivia pays with his life for his sexual excesses and jealousy. Again, illicit love and unbridled ambition are the undoing of the bullfighter Juan Gallardo in *The Blood of the Arena.* And in *Luna Benamor* Blasco shows another resolution to the question of intermarriage where though love may conquer, its victory cannot do away with ancient tradition. Whereas these psychological novels did little to advance Blasco's literary standing, they continued to buttress his popular and Hollywood fame—*The Blood of the Arena* will be remembered mostly as Rudolph Valentino's famous film debut.

The publication of *The Four Horsemen of the Apocalypse* in 1916 ended a six-year silence for Blasco the novelist and marked the beginning of a new cycle of novels, a trilogy called the "cosmopolitan novels." With the other two, *Mare Nostrum (Our Sea,* 1918) and *Los enemigos de la mujer (The Enemies of Women,* 1919), they are also known as the "European novels" because they concern themselves with World War I. Whether taken singly or as a trilogy these works have little literary merit, but for a time they (especially *The Four Horsemen of the Apocalypse*) were Blasco's most widely read works, responsible for his growing worldwide fame. The 1921 film version of this novel (remade in 1962 with Glen Ford and Charles Boyer) made a star of Rudolph Valentino, much the same as the 1923 screen version of *The Enemies of Women* did for Lionel Barrymore. *Our Sea* (as the Romans called the Mediterranean) was also filmed twice, in 1926 in the United States and in Mexico in 1948. Today it is hardly believable that such attention and importance should have been attached to these works. *The Four Horsemen of the Apocalypse,* a vague attempt to portray the whole of World War I, comes across as little more than a work of propaganda for the Allied cause, thus giving credence to the story of French President Poincare's personally asking Blasco to use the Battle of the Marne as an inspiration for a novel depicting the ravages of war. The novel does focus on the comings and goings of Paris intellectuals, the moneyed, and the armed forces, showing how wartime affects them all from the vantage point of an emigrated Argentine family. It is a pessimistic outlook on humankind. *Our Sea* shifts the scene of the conflict from French soil to the underwater action of submarine warfare, dramatizing vividly the terrible evils of the modern war machine, which causes so much death and destruction, exemplified by German submarines. *The Enemies of Women* transports the reader to the glittering world of Monte Carlo where the aristocratic set, a group of jaded and pleasure-loving characters, seeks to insulate themselves from the 1914–18 conflict. Given the statement "I produce my novels according to the milieu in which I live,"[13] this last novel speaks eloquently as to Blasco's elevated position in European society.

The largest group of novels to come from Blasco's pen was that of "historical narratives." His first work of fiction belonged to this category, as did most of his last ones (some posthumous). Blasco's historical novels bracket the rest of his production. There are, then, two historical epochs. The first one is made up mostly of short novelettes published in the years 1888–92, written in the manner of Fernández y González's potboilers, meant to entertain their readers and sell newspapers befitting their nature of serialized novels. These romances, not unlike present-day comic books or soap operas, contain plenty of action, romance, and intrigue. Historical settings and events fall victim to more appealing heroes and their improbable deeds. *El conde Fernán González* is the first in this group of some twenty volumes which not even Blasco himself wanted preserved for posterity—they have been duly excluded from every complete works edition. The second epoch of historical novels differs from the first in that history no longer appears romanticized. Blasco in this second part of the series endeavors to reconstruct historical episodes and reevaluate characters seeking to bring to light, through painstaking documentation, new and interesting facets heretofore unknown or untold.

Almost every one of the four books that comprise the cycle strives for the revindication of notable historical figures who in some way had been vilified in the past. In *The Pope of the Sea,* the spotlight is on Benedict XIII, Avignon pope during the Church schism. *A los pies de Venus (At the Feet of Venus,* 1926) chronicles the papacy of the Borgias, the Valencian family (née Borja) of notorious Catholic leaders, thus in a sense continuing the saga of *The Pope of the Sea. En busca del Gran Kan (Unknown Lands,* 1928) tells of Christopher Columbus's mistaken notion of his reaching China and India in his first voyage of discovery of the Americas. The last work of this group, *El caballero de la Virgen (Knight of the Virgin,* 1929) recalls the adventures of the conqueror Alonso de Ojeda who died alone and a pauper after having provided land, people, and untold riches for Spain. There exists a thread of narrative progression running through all of these novels. Chronologically, beginning in 1394 when Pedro de Luna became Pope Benedict XIII through the death of the explorer Ojeda in 1519, Blasco takes the reader on a historical tour of Spain, the Catholic church in Europe, the voyages of Columbus and his lieutenant Ojeda, and the latter's wanderings on the new continent. The breadth of this panorama, as well as its carefully researched background, more than makes up for the often-cited museumlike tone that for some critics damns these historical narratives.

Equally lengthy but grander in scale was to have been another series of novels projected by Blasco, but World War I cut it short after only one volume had been issued, *Los Argonautas* (1914). After the conclusion of the war, Blasco's own death again reduced it to two volumes, *La tierra de todos (The Temptress,* 1922) and *La reina Calafia (Queen Calafia,* 1923). This series, to be called "American novels," was inspired by Blasco's six-year adventure in South America, where he did everything from delivering speeches to climbing mountains and founding colonies at the behest of foreign governments. A man of action, Blasco perhaps fantasized on becoming a conquistador of history and legend. Economic turmoil and the advent of World War I, however, put an end to the city settlements of Nueva Valencia and Cervantes in the Argentine *pampa,* forcing

Blasco to return to his reality as a writer. Nevertheless, he wished to immortalize not so much what he himself had done in America but the deeds of his ancestors and to glorify the beauty and the grandeur of the new continent. His epic of the Americas was begun by *Los Argonautas,* a long drawn-out account of the coming to Buenos Aires of Fernando de Ojeda and his travels through South America. A sequel to this work was never finished; instead he wrote *The Temptress,* set in a newly colonized region of Argentina and centering on a femme fatale who, having destroyed countless lives as the dominant force in Río Negro, ends her days as a streetwalker. Aware of his deftness as a novelist, Hollywood producers could not pass up such a melodramatic plot and it was made into a film vehicle for Greta Garbo in 1926. *Queen Calafia,* a story set in California that loosely parallels in a modern setting the apocryphal account of the queen of the same name in the knight-errant book *Las sergas de Esplandián (The exploits of Espandián)* written by Garci Ordóñez de Montalvo in 1510 and one of Don Quixote's favorites, puts an end to the American novels. Blasco had five and perhaps six more narratives in mind when death overtook him on 28 January, 1928. The titles he had planned were "La ciudad de la esperanza" (The city of hope) about Buenos Aires, "Los murmullos de la selva" (The murmurs of the jungle) about the uncivilized territories, "El oro y la muerte" (Gold and death) about Perú, and two, possibly three, more devoted to the Chilean region.

Vicente Blasco Ibáñez's considerable novelistic output is diverse, popular, and literarily meritorious and influential. His best came at the beginning with the works grouped under the heading "regional novels." Later on, even if he fell out of favor with critics of literature on account of his facile, propagandist, and melodramatic writings, Blasco was adopted by the largest readership any modern Spanish author had known in his day. He is probably the first Spaniard to become an international best-seller and certainly the only one whose books were widely transformed into motion pictures. To this day Blasco remains one of Spain's greatest storytellers and a figure often larger than life.

Chapter Two

Miguel de Unamuno: The Existentialist Novel

The year 1898, date of Spain's defeat at the hands of the United States and the loss of her last colonies, signals the beginning of the country's modern era. So, even though historically and politically 1898 is highly significant, in the realm of letters—with the exception of the publication of Blasco Ibáñez's *La barraca (The Cabin)*—strictly speaking the year holds no special importance for Spanish literature. In a broader context, however, the date marks the birth of a group of writers who in the next quarter century would produce a body of literature so new and varied that it rivals Spain's sixteenth- and seventeenth-century Golden Age.

The Generation of 1898

The members of this most famous generation in Spanish literature are Ramón María del Valle Inclán (1866–1936), José Martínez Ruiz, better known as "Azorín" (1873–1967), Pío Baroja y Nessi (1872-1956), Miguel de Unamuno y Jugo (1864-1936), Ramiro de Maeztu (1874–1936), and Antonio Machado (1875–1939). The acrostic VABUMM!, made up from the initials of their last names, constitutes onomatopoeically the impression they sought to convey to their contemporaries—a big bang. Theirs was a rebellious attitude voiced in protests and in their stand against traditional ways. At the inception of the Generation its closest members, politically speaking, were Unamuno, Azorín, Baroja and Maeztu, but as they matured, all esprit de corps vanished, and the original political focus gradually changed to a literary one. Their disbandment occurred around 1905 although the label "Generation of 1898" did not appear until 1913. Azorín popularized the designation in four articles, titled "La Generación de 1898," written for the Madrid daily *ABC* in February of that year, so that its conscious naming came long after its factual dissolution. Spain's immediate political and social plight had ceased to be the essential theme of their writings ex-cepting those of Maeztu, for whom these subjects remained the only constant. Slowly and tentatively at first, but with a decided and irrevocable attitude, each author turned in his own direction and, as he gained confidence and stature, began giving free rein to his individual ethical and aesthetic preferences.

They had been drawn together initially by coinciding birthdates (all were born within ten years of each other and three died in the same year), similar education and upbringing (most were self-edu-cated), a historical event creating a state of collective awareness (the disastrous defeat of 1898), a common language, a common leader (Unamuno), and shared experiences (close personal contact in news-rooms, political protests, and cafés). Each tried to stand out from the group from the very beginning: Azorín wore a monocle and carried a red umbrella, Unamuno dressed as a Protestant pastor, Valle Inclán let his beard grow waist-long and pinned up his coat sleeve in order to make more obvious the loss of his left arm, Baroja wore a Basque beret and a dark overcoat even inside his apartment, Machado's unkempt appearance typified his rural schoolteacher's low salary, and Maeztu's conservative British gentleman's attire belied his unpredictable behavior. In time their histrionic poses changed to more meaningful belletristic differentiations and their uniqueness derived from their writings rather than from their mannerisms or garb. Personally they also drifted apart. Their common friend, the journalist José María Salaverría, wrote in one of his articles that "they respected each other though they did not like one another very much. Azorín held Baroja faithfully in high esteem, and that is as far as the congeniality went. Maeztu was jealous of Azorín and detested Baroja. Baroja could not stand Unamuno and Unamuno did not care for anybody."[1] Baroja in his *Memorias* (Memoirs) says that Maeztu and Azorín once came close to blows since "Maeztu was always on the verge of provoking conflicts because his claims were so exaggerated that no one could listen to them calmly."[2] Maeztu grew more and more disillusioned with his friends as one by one they all became oblivious to the political scene, an arena he never left.[3] When Baroja went to London where Maeztu worked as a foreign correspondent for several Madrid newspapers, the latter did not even want to see him. Baroja, as a result, came to feel a deep dislike for Maeztu. They last saw each other at the end of 1935 when Baroja went on a trip to his native Basque country. On the way he met Unamuno, and on the trip back he chanced upon Maeztu, both Basques also, in the same railway car. Wrote Baroja: "Had I known it, I would have avoided them both, and, possibly, they would have done the same with me."[4]

In the end it mattered little what each thought of the others' politics. Their political accomplishments were rendered fruitless. Maeztu was shot as a political prisoner, Unamuno died while under house arrest, Machado died in political exile, and all had run-ins with the authorities at one time or another. It is their literary work that remains uppermost. Thanks to it and to these six magnificent literary personalities, the originally negative significance of the year 1898 became a proud date in the cultural history of Spain.

Existentialism and Unamuno

Existentialism, far from being the firm doctrine thought by many, is instead a loosely conceived, understood, and practical set of humanistic and philosophical tendencies so broad that, on an ethical plane, it allows for the existence of God (Kierkegaard, Jaspers, Marcel) at one extreme, and at the other vehemently denies it (Heidegger, Sartre, Camus). Though such early thinkers as Saint Augustine (354–430), in his *Confessions,* and Blaise Pascal (1623–62), in his *Pensées (Thoughts),* have been considered by some as forerunners of existentialism by virtue of their works' penetrating self-analyses, undeniably the true exponents of modern existentialism are the philosophers Sören Kierkegaard (1813–55), Friedrich Nietzsche (1844–1900), and Martin Heidegger (1889–) among the most prominent. Whereas the Danish theologian Kierkegaard accepted the existence of God and even the divinity of Christ, both Nietzsche and Heidegger declare God's absence from the world. The former pronounced him dead since there can be no place for an immutable God in a universe that is always becoming and therefore changing; the latter protested his own atheism in spite of an absent God. But while many of existentialism's adherents differ among themselves concerning a resolution or even an interpretation of the most fundamental dilemmas in man's existence, they hold certain beliefs in common. First, that "existence precedes essence," meaning that man exists before he starts to become an individual by dint of his own actions, be they chosen instinctively, deliberately, or subconsciously. Thus, every man is a unique, self-fashioned individual, never complete or set but, rather, forever changing. Second, that man is free and able to choose, a property that may lead to anxiety when he is forced to make decisions. Third, that man is accosted by feelings of paradox and even guilt over the unpredictability of a purposeless or a godless universe. Fourth, that man's suffering derives from an awareness of certain death in an existence bounded definitively by birth and death. Other themes of existentialism, some corollaries of the foregoing, are alienation, despair, nihilism, absurdity, uncertainty, disillusionment, and self-questioning.

Unamuno, who learned Danish so that he could read Kierkegaard in the original, as he did with all of the other philosophers, fits somewhere in the middle of existentialism's spectrum, both as an author and as a thinker. The Spaniard neither denied nor affirmed the existence of God. Unable rationally to prove or disprove it, Unamuno doubted it. In his fiction he substitutes imagination for reason, creating a scenario in which a dialectic between sentiment and reason unfolds in differing versions, what Karl Jaspers (1883–1969) calls "boundary situations." In Unamuno's case, as in those of other existentialist authors such as Camus (1913–60), these are extreme, intense, or critical moments and periods in the lives of the protagonists of his novels. Prior to Unamuno, no other writer in Spain had invoked such forces in his fiction. Only foreign authors, such as the Russian Dostoevski (1821–91) with whom he has often been compared, share in the Spaniard's dramatic, passionate, and fateful mode of writing. The tragic sense of life—as Unamuno titled one of his nonfiction volumes—that both Unamuno and Dostoevski infuse into their works through their tormented characters and the passions that dominate them, the role that fate plays, and the limit-situations that inevitably lead to their demise, support the contention that Unamuno should be considered among the first of the existentialist novelists of our time.[5]

The Life of Miguel de Unamuno

In the Basque city of Bilbao, in northern Spain, Miguel de Una-amuno y Jugo de Larraza was born on 29 September, 1864, to the shopkeeper Félix de Unamuno and his wife Salomé de Jugo. The third of six children, he was baptized with the name of the saint of the day, Saint Michael, who as the writer was later to point out means "who like God"—foreboding of one who questioned God's own existence. Raised in the midst of a traditional Catholic family, the young Miguel first attended a private school and then moved on to the Instituto Vizcaíno, the public high school of Bilbao where the comings and goings of troops and the daily bombardments of enemy fire made learning a difficult task. On 28 October, 1873 the second Carlist War began. The elder Unamuno, Don Félix, had died three years earlier when Miguel was barely six. It fell to the mother to provide for and bring up all of the children on her own. Alone without a father, the young Unamuno started his lifelong habit of reading voraciously. Ensconced in the small library that his father had put together while seeking his fortune in Mexico, Miguel discovered the pleasures of reading and made his first acquaintances with select works that included not only literary masterpieces such as Cervantes's *Don Quixote,* but also the philosophical treatises of Jaime Balmes (1810–48) and the lives of saints.

Since Unamuno's favorite subject, when writing, was himself and he wrote constantly, resulting in a complete works collection of considerable volume, it follows that this early period of his life eventually appeared both in his fiction and nonfiction. In the *Recuerdos de niñez y mocedad* (Remembrances of childhood and adolescence) Unamuno provides us with a good-humored autobiography of his early years in Bilbao, and in *Paz en la guerra (Peace in War,* 1897), the fictionalized persona Pachico Zababilde re-creates the intimate crisis that befell the author, his family, and the rest of his native city during the Carlist siege.

Having completed his *bachillerato* (high school) studies and written his first newspaper article,[6] Unamuno left for Madrid at age sixteen to enroll at the University in the College of Filosofía y Letras (liberal arts). There he led a life of austerity and study; he did not drink— except a glass of wine with meals—or smoke, and did not keep company with women. He also stopped going to church when, after having missed mass one Sunday, he discovered that it made little difference to him whether he went again or not. In 1884 he received his doctoral degree in letters with a thesis on the Basque language that was finally published in the 1970s. Unhappy and rather homesick, Unamuno returned to Bilbao after a distinguished university career to prepare for the *oposiciones* (nationally held competitive examinations) that he hoped would yield a tenured professorship in a university somewhere in Spain. While studying for these examinations, Unamuno gave private lessons, taught part-time at his old high school, and continued to write for the local paper, *El noticiero bilbaíno,* mostly under the pseudonym "Yo mismo" ("I myself"). On 25 October, 1886 his first short story, "Ver con los ojos" (Through my own eyes), appeared in this newspaper with the customary pen name. As it turns out, it was based on his love affair with Concepción (Concha) Lizárraga, whom he married on 31 January, 1891, the same year in which he finally succeeded in securing a *cátedra* (teaching chair) at the University of Salamanca as professor of Greek language and literature. Unaccountably for someone of his intellect and dedication, Unamuno for three years had tried and failed to obtain professorships first in logic, then in metaphysics, and finally in Latin.

In the month of June 1891 Unamuno and his wife first set foot in Salamanca, a university city of only 23,000 inhabitants, that neither would leave permanently for the rest of their lives. He began his duties as professor and chairman of the Greek department in October 1891 and settled down to a life of teaching and writing, a routine that lasted for nine years, when he was appointed "Rector magnífico" (university president) of the university. The raise in salary plus the use of a rent-free house provided by the University of Salamanca for its president meant that Unamuno, burdened with six children, no longer had to occupy so many hours penning newspaper articles to supplement his meager income. He continued to lead a life of personal frugality and self-denial where his only expenses were for a few travels and the purchase of books—when he died his library had in the vicinity of six thousand volumes. His dress of dark navy blue was the same summer and winter, save only the gloves as a concession to the cold—he owned no overcoat—and by this time he had given up even wine as his sole indulgence.

With his appointment to the presidency, a political charge as much as an academic one, Unamuno's involvement in public affairs grew beyond the city of Salamanca. Gray-bearded with his hair thinning, the thirty-six-year-old university president faced crises within his own university and disputes outside of it, mainly with the central government in Madrid, which did not always agree with Unamuno's strictly ethical decisions to the detriment of political considerations. Though pressured by various groups to become a member of one political party or another, Unamuno recoiled before the idea. He would fight for causes, but without any party affiliation. As a result he campaigned, made speeches, and wrote articles that at one time made it seem as though he was a militant socialist and at another a republican sympathizer.

With few allies in Salamanca, and embattled by political, academic, and literary envies as well as attempts to discredit him, Unamuno felt his health deteriorate as he developed angina pectoris. One of his children (the mongoloid Raimundín) died, he began to doubt his success as a teacher, and he considered leaving Salamanca for Madrid but, mired down in the provincial city, he gave up the idea for good. These were years (1897–1915) when—more conscious than ever of his own mortality—Unamuno began writing poetry and laying the groundwork for his key philosophical treatise *El sentimiento trágico de la vida* (*The Tragic Sense of Life*, 1912). Intellectually Unamuno stayed alive in this recondite city not only through his readings, his writings, and his university teaching but also through dialogues with other men equally devoted to academia, such as the younger Ortega y Gasset. These pursuits soon led him to break with such former associates as Maeztu, to ignore others like Baroja, and, eventually, Azorín, and to disdain the rest, among them Valle Inclán.

In the fall of 1914 Unamuno was removed as president of the University by the minister of public education. His plans to travel to South America felled by this purely political maneuver, Unamuno returned to his old teaching schedule—now Spanish philology as well as Greek—and curtailed all outside activities that did not coincide with holidays or vacation periods in order to fulfill his duties as professor punctiliously and avoid criticism of any sort. In spite of his diminished role, Unamuno's name continued appearing in newspapers all over Spain in the guise of newsmaker as much as the author of an article or a short story. Neither fame nor notoriety, however, sufficed to restrain the dictatorship of General Miguel Primo de Rivera from dismissing Unamuno from his tenured post and exiling him (for a series of articles written years earlier against the monarchy) to the island of Fuerteventura off the coast of West Africa.

This forced exile became a voluntary one when, after five months, Unamuno was pardoned on 4 July, 1924 but decided to continue his fight against the Primo de Rivera rule from France. Taken to Paris from Fuerteventura by the publisher of the paper *Le Quotidien* in a chartered yacht, Unamuno soon tired of life in the French capital where he had been paraded by his liberator and other ac-

quaintances as Spain's premier individualist and fighter of the op-
position. Only his sometime friend Vicente Blasco Ibáñez helped
to relieve Unamuno from the tedium of his metropolitan existence
and the nostalgia for his beloved Spain. Rainer Maria Rilke, Alfonso
Reyes, Jean Cassou, John Galsworthy, Paul Valéry, Luigi Piran-
dello, and James Joyce, among others, were writers with whom he
had some contact during his stay in Paris. Their company was not
enough to dissuade him from leaving, and on 28 August, 1925,
Unamuno settled in the small town of Hendaye, in the French
Pyrenees, from where he could actually see Spain.

Six years later, after Primo de Rivera's fall, Unamuno returned
to Spain expecting to resume a normal life in Salamanca. The public
acclaim with which he was welcomed back precluded any such
normalcy. Instead of settling into an academic career, Unamuno
was impelled into a public one. His penchant for speaking out and
his international stature made him not only a celebrity but an issue
wherever he went and whatever he said. More than once he was
ushered out of Madrid by the police, and many of his newspaper
articles were suppressed by government censors, but Unamuno re-
taliated by publishing his diatribes outside of Spain in such prestigious dailies as the *New York Times.*[7] The Spanish government
realized that it could not gag Unamuno and, in an effort to control
him, appointed him minister of public education on 27 April, 1931
and a few weeks later reinstated him as president of the University
of Salamanca. These honors together with Unamuno's election to
the Spanish *Cortes* (Spanish Parliament) and the Royal Academy of
Letters, testimonies to the power of his intellect and incorruptible
dedication to principled beliefs, were deserving merits for an aging
warrior—a realization made more evident by the deaths of his brother
Fernando, his sisters Susana and María, two of his children, his
wife, Concha, his intimate friend the blind poet Rodríguez Pinilla,
and even some of his former favorite students. Unamuno began to
feel old and, in spite of public attention, more alone as the years
went by. When the time for his retirement arrived, the citizens of
Salamanca crowded into Unamuno's classroom to listen to his last
lecture. After a few weeks of forced idleness with time heavy upon
him, Unamuno traveled once more to Portugal, England, and
throughout Spain, returning for the last time to Salamanca where
two months before his death, under house arrest, on 31 December,

1936, Francisco Franco decreed Unamuno's final dismissal as president of Salamanca's university.

Literature and Unamuno's Novels

Unamuno was not only the most prolific but the most protean author of his generation. The fame and output of his pen are diversely distributed among the essay, drama, poetry, journalism, and the novel. The sole belletristic pursuit in which he did not engage was literary criticism, despising the whole idea. Because his was an intellectual closet drama devoid of all action, Unamuno largely failed in the theater. As an essayist, he excelled because the amorphousness of the genre's limits suited his temperament well. He began to write poetry late in life—he was forty-three years old when his first book of verse, *Poesías* (Poems), appeared in 1907—but as he grew older Unamuno wrote little else, devoting to it the last three or four years of his life. He wrote in newspapers and magazines primarily for two reasons: to earn a supplemental income with which to support his large family and to vent publicly his sociopolitical and literary views, which were many and always controversial.

Not only to the critic of the novel but also to the literary critic in general Unamuno's novelistic output appears to be his greatest contribution to modern literature. The reason is twofold: he is an innovator, and his novel incarnates the strongest tenets of his life and thought. First of all, Unamuno's novel is new in the sense that he stripped it of all the traditional nineteenth-century trappings (long descriptive passages, sagalike complicated relationships, and expanded chronological dimensions), compressing it into a dense, single-minded narrative so lacking in detail that only dialogue seems to have survived. In this way he fashioned a novel that deals almost exclusively with one or two characters—sometimes in a schizophrenic way (e.g., *Abel Sánchez*)—and one or two essential passionate dilemmas on which their lives hinge. This personal novel[8] was the forerunner of the existentialist novel wherein the set of alternatives confronting the protagonist—literally the "first against" or struggler in its etymological sense as Unamuno saw it—are made to symbolize those of man in general. Indeed, in more than one of Unamuno's novels, but especially *Niebla (Mist)*, published in 1914, the very existence of the main character becomes the essence of the work. These became known as *nivolas*, a label invented by Unamuno himself when accused of writing novels so unorthodox. Second, Unamuno found the novel to be a way to satisfy both his aesthetic drive (very minor if one is to believe the author's own words) and his metaphysical longings (all-consuming, judging by the endless variations of the same themes and their omnipresence).

Two overriding concerns stand out in all of Unamuno's production regardless of genre: the concept of *intrahistoria* and his contest with death. The former refers to his preoccupation with individual man, who struggles with life and time in a dimension less heroic than history but which ultimately constitutes its basic ingredient. *Intrahistoria* refers to what is inside history, its smallest component, which on account of its inevitability achieves an undeniable significance. Each segment of *intrahistoria* may go unnoticed or unsung but without it history would be devoid of all meaning. The novel *Peace in War* best exemplifies this concept, which Unamuno had formerly introduced in the collection of essays *En torno al casticismo* (On authentic tradition) years earlier.

Anguished by a lifelong preoccupation with immortality, Unamuno envisioned the road to reason closed by death. The novel opened a new road via the imagination. Unamuno sought to make the novel a stage where he could, if not solve, at least play out to his own satisfaction all of the possibilities raised by the haunting despair that death meant for him. Unamuno was confronted by one question that could only result in a philosophical dilemma. Paraphrased it would be: If I don't die (i.e., completely, meaning there is life after death), what will become of me? If, on the other hand, I do die (i.e., completely, meaning no hereafter), then nothing makes sense.[9] Life loses interest for Unamuno if it is not eternal because, for him, death means final defeat. His most famous novel, *Mist,* and his last narrative, *San Manuel Bueno, mártir (Saint Manuel Bueno, Martyr),* are animated by such a tragic sense, each unfolding it differently but ending in the same way.

Because Unamuno's novels do not fit into one clearly existentialist or personal category, I have divided his longest narratives, about twelve, into three clearly distinguishable classifications: traditional, unorthodox, and moral. The traditional novels, those written in customary format with narration, description, and dialogue, are his first and his last: *Peace in War* and *Saint Manuel Bueno, Martyr,* 1897 and 1931 respectively. The unorthodox novels or *nivolas,* essayistic works, whose characters are little more than ideas, are *Amor y pedagogía*

(Love and education, 1902), *Mist,* and *Nada menos que todo un hombre*
(Every inch a man, 1916). The morality novels, tales of passion
lacking spatial or temporal dimensions—like the *nivolas*—are *Abel
Sánchez* (1917), *La tía Tula* (Aunt Gertrude, 1921), and *La novela
de Don Sandalio, jugador de ajedrez (The Novel of Don Sandalio, Chessplayer,* 1930).

The Traditional Novels

When he had finished his university studies in 1885, Unamuno
began writing a novel that would take him twelve years to complete.
Peace in War remained unfinished until the summer of 1896 and
unpublished until the following year.

Given Unamuno's philosophical disposition, it is not difficult to
see why his first and his last novels are of the same sort. In *Peace
in War,* Unamuno's moral debts are to his Roman Catholic domestic
upbringing, his aesthetic ones to the realist novels of Benito Pérez
Galdós. At the end of his life, though much modified by many
literary, social, political, and religious experiences, Unamuno has
come almost full circle. *Peace in War* and *Saint Manuel Bueno, Martyr*
possess a shared theme (individual and eternal life), a similar final
resolution (consolation through acceptance of the inevitable), and
the same chronological unfolding (death as the end only to individual
life). Between these two works Unamuno had tested both metaphysical and aesthetic methods without finding satisfaction. In the
end he finished where he had begun, but the search had not been
fruitless because he had found that there was no answer other than
those principles that had initially motivated his search. If Unamuno
had not found a way to either prove or disprove them, then he
would have had to content himself with the knowledge that there
was no answer to the question "Is there a life after death?" The
thirty-four-year-long novelistic search, a way of life for Unamuno,
yielded as its testimony the replete volumes of his complete works.
Paradoxically, this inquiry, though a failure in a philosophical sense,
conferred upon its author an immortality in the literary sense. For
Unamuno this may not have been enough, even though he must
have known at the end that he had to be content with it—Unamuno
the man was to die; Unamuno the writer would endure.

On more than one occasion Unamuno declared that every truly

original novel had to be autobiographical.[10] Whether or not he made such a declaration because he believed it was true for everyone else's novels since such was the case with his own, remains unclear; his are all thoroughly and demonstrably autobiographical. Indeed, the sole subject and object not only of his novels but of all his fiction as well as poetry and a great deal of his nonfictional works was Unamuno himself—the man of flesh and blood. In *Saint Manuel Bueno, Martyr,* the country priest personifies Unamuno's dilemma. In *Peace in War* two characters, Ignacio Iturriondo and Pachico Zababilde, incarnate successive stages in the author's emotional and spiritual evolution.

Peace in War, a title likely suggested by Leo Tolstoy's *War and Peace* (1862–69) or P.J. Proudhon's *La guerre et la paix* (War and peace, 1861), is not only Unamuno's first published[11] novel but also his longest. Written in a *tempo lento* (slow narrative) fashion, *Peace in War* recalls the years 1874–76 of the second Carlist War, experienced day to day by a few intimately portrayed characters. The narrative process responds to Unamuno's concept of *intrahistoria* where the fundamental strata of history are layered. Ignacio, like his father, Pedro Antonio, before him in the first Carlist War, fights for the traditionalist cause although he neither understands it too well nor is fully convinced of its righteousness. Ignacio's death, like that of others, particularly when the conflict is ebbing, therefore seems pointless and as difficult to explain as his unquestioning faith or his blind allegiance to traditional values. Pachico, a young intellectual, fills Ignacio's void and reveals the maturing Unamuno in a coming to grips with the dialectic between war and peace in the life of a man.

For Unamuno everyday life, full of routines and monotony, constitutes man's most meaningful reality. Though war is passing and peace is what remains, both are equally necessary in terms of history. As far as man is concerned, he can find peace in war since his own life amounts to nothing more than a series of unchronicled incidents and accidents—the meat of *intrahistoria*—that may finally add up to a historical footnote. Ignacio's death, useless in the end and even unknown to some like Pachico, becomes integrated into a natural order that dictates that death and war are essential contrapuntal dimensions of life and peace. One cannot be understood without the other. In this novel of space and time, the progression of themes is, on the one hand, one of *intrahistoria,* history, and eternity; and, on the other, one of individual man, life, and nature. *Peace in War* ends on the hopeful note of Pachico's final contemplation, but equally implied is a melancholy consideration alluding to man's own mortal makeup that in future works will become all-consuming.

Saint Manuel Bueno, Martyr, Unamuno's most perfect work and his shortest full-length novel, tells the story of a village priest whose own lack of belief in eternal life does not prevent him from preaching to his flock about the promise of Heaven. Writing in November 1930, a few years before his death, Unamuno crystallizes poetically in *Saint Manuel* his own lasting spiritual torment over whether or not there is life after death. The dilemma is played out in this novelette without forcing a solution, which to Unamuno's mind probably does not exist. The protagonist Manuel Bueno dies without knowing what awaits on the other side of death's threshold.

The fiction piece approaches poetry in its synthetic and lyrical expression. Compact, symbolic, and nostalgic, *Saint Manuel* is narrated retrospectively in the first person by Angela (meaning "messenger of God"), one of Manuel (Immanuel: in Hebrew, "Messiah") Bueno's (in Spanish: "Good"; *mártir* in Greek, "witness") disciples—the other one is Lazarus, her brother—and a native of the village of Renada (re-nata, meaning "born again") where for forty years, since Angela was ten until she died after fifty, Don Manuel cares for his parishioners with an authority that is uncommon for a country priest.

The small community of Valverde de Lucerna is an isolated village where this Catholic priest finds consolation in helping others believe what he himself doubts—the immortality of man's soul. Forever afraid of being idle or alone—lest he meditate and fall into a metaphysical despair—Manuel sacrifices his life for the sake of others, encouraging them to marry, helping them feed themselves, lending a hand with their daily chores, and above all teaching them to love one another. Manuel's teachings, far from being steeped in theology or even religion, derive from a fundamental acceptance that one's existence must be led as though there were no other life—that today counts as much as any tomorrow. Reality, necessity, and sincerity in Valverde de Lucerna constantly upstage the traditional Catholic canons of faith and life everlasting.

Unamuno completes the tight symbolic framework of *Saint Manuel* begun through the apellative characterization by providing a remote, rural setting whose most enigmatic landmarks are the mountain and the lake that encircle Valverde (i.e., *valle verde,* "green valley") de Lucerna (i.e., *luz eterna,* "eternal light"). The mountain, rising toward the sky, represents the blind faith of Manuel's flock, their prayers, and their belief in Heaven. The priest's own words of worship "would fall onto the lake and at the foot of the mountain,"[12] suggesting that Manuel's offering does not have the valid sincerity of the others'. The lake, where an older Valverde lies buried underwater in a telling *intrahistorical* note, represents more poignantly Manuel's troubled spirit. As the priest watches the snow falling into the lake and its flakes dissolve and become part of the water, rather than remaining whole and accumulating palpably as they do when settling on the mountain, Manuel comes to a self-realization that is Unamuno's own. Each flake falling into the lake represents one man's death through which the individual becomes part of the greater whole or universe. This is the crux of Miguel de Unamuno's own dilemma, his objection (already voiced in *The Tragic Sense of Life*) to death's being the absorption of man into an immense amalgam that totally erases his uniqueness. Unamuno's resistance is not to death but rather to the annihilation of his individual self. He wanted desperately to continue being Miguel (i.e., "¿Quién como Dios?"—"Who is like God?")[13] after life. The doctrine of St. Paul known as "apocatastasis" (in which all things revert to God) or "anacefaleosis" (in which all creatures revert to Christ),[14] amounting to the surrender or loss of individual consciousness, was feared by Unamuno to be the likeliest resolution of man's destiny since it meant his own disappearance as a unique being. The initial sentence of his *Recuerdos de niñez y mocedad,* "Yo no me acuerdo de haber nacido" ("I do not remember being born"),[15] tells of Unamuno's existential conviction that in that state of universal consciousness— where man exists as an undistinguishable part of a greater whole— there can be no awareness of one's own existence. Thus his reason told him, yet his heart consoled him with the doubt that it was possible for things to be otherwise.

The Novel as a Morality Play

Because of the predominance of dialogue, action, and passion to the detriment of narration, description, and interiorization, the novels *Abel Sánchez* and *La tía Tula* truly approach the nature of drama. The former, subtitled "Una historia de pasión" ("A Story of Passion"), is more specifically, as Unamuno conceded in the prologue to the second edition, the story of one passion: envy. In essence, *Abel Sánchez* unfolds in a timeless, though recognizably modern setting, the biblical story of Cain and Abel—a story whose crime (fratricide) and passion (envy or jealousy) Unamuno believed to be particularly applicable to Spaniards.[16] The title *Abel Sánchez,* also the protagonist's name, joins the biblical name Abel to one of the most common everyday Spanish last names—Sánchez—implying an "everyman" whose long ascendancy dates back to the Bible. The antagonist Joaquín—rhymes consonantally with Caín—has as his own revealing last name, Monegro (monte negro), meaning a "mountain of blackness."

In the unfolding of *Abel Sánchez* the reader slowly becomes aware of Unamuno's inability to understand God's preference for Abel over his brother Cain and his own sympathy for Cain's lot. At times it is easy to believe that Unamuno thought that God was responsible for Cain's crime since he had incited envy in the breast of the killer by accepting Abel's offering over his brother's. As a result, *Abel Sánchez* depicts a tormented Joaquín (a man of science and therefore one who has had to study to become what he is, a physician) as he tries to compete with Abel (an artist and therefore one who was given his talent) from almost before they were born[17] until the latter is killed by the former. The intertwining of their lives becomes so total that at times one is tempted to think of both as a single character with a schizophrenic reality. Symbolically, the first deity to reject Joaquín in favor of Abel is Helena—the unusual spelling in Spanish (normally Elena) serves to remind the reader of the Greek beauty of the same name. Though Joaquín's cousin, she behaves as a true "belle dame sans merci" (fatal woman)[18] toward him, choosing to marry Abel instead.

Consumed by an envy that is his lifeblood and unable to rid himself of it, Joaquín marries and predicates his existence on Abel's own, hoping to satiate a hate he cannot help. His daughter Joaquina marries Abel's son, Abelín, who chooses to be a doctor like Joaquín—enough of a victory for most men. However, Joaquín, inescapably poisoned by a Cain-like envy, ends the elder Abel's life in spite of himself when the latter suffers a heart attack during a quarrel between the two of them. As he had done in *Saint Manuel,* Unamuno plays out in *Abel Sánchez* another of his life's bêtes noires. Here it is the sin of envy and his own inability to justify Jehova's biblical and overt favoritism of Abel over Cain. This incomprehension led him to portray Joaquín as a victim of his god rather than as an assassin of his brother. The uniqueness of the portrayal elevates *Abel Sánchez* beyond a mere retelling of the Old Testament episode and lends it a modern day relevancy.

In *La tía Tula,* published in 1921, Unamuno fictionalizes maternity as an overwhelming passion. The character that incarnates such an instinct to an abnormal degree is the Aunt Tula of the title, a paradoxical woman who hungers for motherhood while despising men for their sexual appetites. Maternity, conceived as a spiritual inclination totally devoid of a carnal dimension, is enacted in a closed family setting involving Tula, her sister Rosa, and the latter's husband, Ramiro. Instinct (sexuality) versus reason (filial love) is the conflict that unfolds among these characters as the scant narrative interest of *La tía Tula* leads toward another foreseeable ending.

Outwardly another "belle dame sans merci" for Ramiro and, as in Helena's case, stronger than the men she fascinates, Tula holds more interest for her sister Rosa's suitor than does his future bride. Rosa, younger and more beautiful, had been Ramiro's first choice, but now taken by Tula's magnetic presence, he realizes he would rather marry her. Though perhaps in love with Ramiro, Tula not only rejects his advances, but also forces him to marry Rosa. When she dies at childbirth, presenting a new opportunity for her sister to marry Ramiro, Tula once again spurns him and elects instead to care for his children while driving the wretched man into a second marriage with an ordinary woman—the maid Manuela—who also dies not long before Ramiro, leaving Tula, who finally reaches virginal motherhood, to care for all of their children. *La tía Tula* contains a familiar leitmotiv in the fiction of Unamuno: characters dominated by a strong will or passion playing out a limit-situation. Ramiro lives in despair desiring Tula and knowing she loves him, yet at the same time being rejected by her in marriage or as a mere sexual partner. Tula lives a life of frustration because in spite of her love for Ramiro she suppresses it, bringing about unhappiness for them both, a state that results in the sterile maternity by proxy to which she has condemned herself.

In the same vein as these novels of passion falls the collection of three short novelettes, published in 1920 under the title of *Tres novelas ejemplares y un prólogo* (Three exemplary novels and a prologue), *El Marqués de Lumbría* (The marquis of Lumbría), *Nada menos que todo un hombre,* and *Dos madres* (Two mothers). All center on unyielding women—Carolina, Julia, and Raquel, respectively—very much aware of their power over the men who seek to possess and love them. Bitterness, recrimination, and loss typify thematically this group of narratives as the male characters are manipulated and just as often victimized by the "belles dames sans merci" with whom they have had the misfortune of falling in love.

A New Novelistic Genre: The Nivola

When one considers that the foregoing series of narratives stretched the novel toward the drama, it should not be too surprising that Unamuno's best-known fictional mode is the type of novel that borders on the essayistic. To this grouping of *nivolas*—as their creator baptized them when their unorthodox format was protested—whose characters are little more than ideas incarnate, belong *Amor y pedagogía, Mist, Cómo se hace una novela (How to Make a Novel,* 1924), and *The Novel of Don Sandalio, Chessplayer.*

Amor y pedagogía represents Unamuno's first attempt at this new type of narrative fiction wherein plot takes a back seat to the novelist's more notable philosophical concerns. In Unamuno's case it meant giving fictional free rein to those life-and-death preoccupations that he considered infinitely more significant than telling stories to entertain his readers. Unamuno sought to disturb them—whenever they were given any consideration at all—rather than amuse or distract them as most other fiction writers of his day did. With *Amor y pedagogía* Unamuno coined the neologism *nivola* (derivative of the novel) to characterize a new kind of novel that has been variously called personal, essayistic, discursive, and ideological. In essence, it comprises all of those modes because it is undoubtedly the forerunner of the now famous existentialist novel where the characters', the author's, and the reader's concerns converge through their humanity. The distinction between creator and creature or author and character is now discarded, especially when the author Unamuno becomes the character Unamuno, as happens in *Mist.*

In *Amor y pedagogía* the author's voice constantly animates the characters in a free, indirect style that leaves no doubt as to who does the talking. This is the story of Avito Carrascal, the protagonist who, considering himself a thinking man, wishes to live life solely according to reason. Thus, when he decides to marry, Avito makes up his mind to wed the most ideally suited (according to his hypotheses) mate. In order that she be compatible and bear him a genius son Avito settles on the "dolico-blonde" type featuring large breasts, wide hips, good appetite, and healthy color. As chance would have it, ironically, Avito falls instead for the "brachi-brunette" kind who has none of the desirable qualities on his list, but who happens to accept his proposal of marriage. This about-face in the first stage of Avito's master plan foretells the successive reversals that make his ideas on love and education unrealizable: his wife, Marina, interferes at every turn, his friend Fulgencio advises him that women are nothing more than raw instinct, and their son Apolodoro hangs himself. This tragicomic novel, aside from ridiculing the pseudoscientific pedagogical practices then in vogue, demonstrates implicitly Unamuno's belief that man's sentiment and instinct overpower his rational capacities. In Avito Carrascal's case the outcome would have been equally disastrous even had he picked the "dolico-blonde" over the "brachi-brunette," since for him to have made the rational choice over the sentimental one would have been impossible—emotion would have won over reason and prevented the right choice.

Mist, likely Unamuno's most famous *nivola* and the only one so subtitled, clearly stages, in the mind of its author, man's thorniest dilemma—the nature of an individual's existence and the relationship that binds a creature to his creator. Unamuno, a professor of Greek (a civilization that chose to see its gods as exemplifying human foibles), would have liked to deal with his god in more direct and anthropomorphic terms. Consequently he conceived *Mist* as a narrative in which to develop a devised equation where he could work out in scale his own relationship with his maker. God was to Unamuno (god:man) as Unamuno was to Augusto Pérez (creator:creature).

The protagonist Augusto, an introspective and indecisive character, lives in a mist of uncertainty following his overprotective mother's death. After a series of mishaps (which the reader may well ascribe to the absence of the dead mother's protection), such as the deception at the hands of the woman he had sought to marry, the failed seduction of his laundress, and the advice of his friend to commit suicide, Augusto begins to doubt his own existence. In order to quiet his anguish Augusto travels to Salamanca to tell Unamuno of his temptation to kill himself. Unamuno warns Augusto that it is impossible since he lives only in the imagination of his creator. The reply that Augusto gives is predictable. It follows, then, that Unamuno may himself be the figment of another author's imagination.

Of all the questions posed by *Mist* the most suggestive is: can a character possess autonomy from his creator? Unamuno's answer in the novel is paradoxical. He does not allow Augusto to commit suicide nor does he himself kill the character. Instead, Augusto dies of a heart attack as the result of a gastronomic binge after returning from Salamanca. And yet there exists ample evidence that Unamuno did fervently believe in a character's autonomy not only from his creator, but even from the work in which he or she had originated. He thought Don Quixote more famous than his creator Cervantes, and so independent of him that Unamuno dared to write another *Vida de don Quijote y Sancho (Our Lord Don Quixote)* in 1905. Moreover, the prologue to *Mist* itself was "written" by no less than another one of its characters, the fictional Víctor Goti who so ill advises Augusto with his mysterious notions about life and suffering. In the end, *Mist* not unexpectedly turns out to be as inconclusive as its title, given Unamuno's discursive mode and honest proposal in the writing of this work. If he wanted to ascertain his God's existence, his power, and the extent of his own autonomy as a man, the quest did not succeed nearly as well metaphysically as literarily.

Of about the same length as *Saint Manuel* is *The Novel of Don Sandalio, Chessplayer.* Structured in epistolary form, this short novel takes Unamuno's denudation of the genre to its *reductio ad absurdum.* In previous works there had been an absence of background, fewer and fewer characters, and chronological and spatial uncertainties. Now in *Don Sandalio* Unamuno has seemingly managed the impossible by taking away the protagonist just as the reader begins to hope he can know him better. Briefly, *Don Sandalio* tells the story, via a series of letters, of the vacationing Felipe who plays chess with a man named Don Sandalio Cuadrado Redondo (Sandalio from Sandalia, i.e., "sandal"; Cuadrado, "square"; Redondo, "round"). There is no other plot and no other narrative interest. Chess playing, though a social pastime, is a silent game where the two players rarely say much to one another. The setting, then, suits Unamuno's purpose admirably. Felipe has to imagine everything about Don Sandalio, who he is, what he does, what he thinks, where he lives, with whom, etc., *and* so does the reader. When after a few days Don Sandalio fails to show up for the daily afternoon game, only to return briefly before disappearing forever, both Felipe and the reader are left in the same quandary. What has become of Don Sandalio and who was he really? The misanthropic Felipe prefers not to know anything about Don Sandalio even when other people wish to volunteer information about him, for example, his son-in-law after the latter's final disappearance. In *Don Sandalio* Unamuno has created a novel without a plot or a protagonist that ultimately speaks eloquently to the lack of genuine communication in man's verbal dealings with his fellowman. How little we know about our neighbors or our friends in spite of seeing and speaking to them every day of our lives seems to be the lesson implicit in this fascinating tale.

While alone in Paris, Unamuno began to write in the summer months of 1925 a strange book whose title, *How to Make a Novel,* may appear misleading to those unacquainted with the work. It has none of the didactic value associated with writing manuals and little, if any, worth as a novel. *How to Make a Novel* is, instead, an autobiographical attempt on Unamuno's part to fictionalize his own existence. Anguished by his exile, not only from his Spanish homeland, but from the Spanish language and his fellow Spaniards, Unamuno thought that he could survive these difficult times in France only by writing himself into his own work. "Here you have me before these blank pages, trying to pour my life into them so that I can keep on living,"[19] he wrote. Short of money, Unamuno had this work translated into French by Jean Cassou so that it could be published in the journal *Mercure de France.*[20] When he later decided he wanted to publish it in Spanish, the original manuscript had been lost, so Unamuno translated it back from the French and added many new paragraphs onto the first version, finally publishing it in Spain in 1927.

How to Make a Novel thus becomes a hybrid work, composed from the most heterogeneous elements: autobiography, confession, fiction, diary, translation, testimony, monologue, commentary, and amplification of itself. It is difficult to classify. Yet two very important facets of *How to Make a Novel* must be taken into account: (1) Unamuno's declaration in it that every truly authentic novel is to a great extent autobiographical in nature,[21] and (2) that the "Novel" mentioned in the title here refers to "life" or "biography," a most significant meaning since the narrator-protagonist is none other than Unamuno himself. Even if *How to Make a Novel* possesses doubtful fictional worth as a novel or nonfictional value as a how-to-manual—arguably in both cases—it further expands the meaning of the genre in Unamunian terms, particularly vis-à-vis his constant and progressive pruning away, from its most ancillary to its most essential elements: from setting and description to narration and elimination of plot, from diminution of characters to lack of protagonist, and ultimately to the complete eclecticism of the genre in *How to Make a Novel.*

With the exception of his first novel, *Peace in War,* all of Unamuno's novels are analytical and personal pieces of fiction, though not so distant from himself and his perennial dilemmas. His characters agonize—"struggle," in the true etymological sense of the word—in a predetermined life stage, all of them devoid of any free will. Introverts to the last, Unamuno's protagonists despair in a pessimism that can be said to mirror almost exclusively their creator's own existential angst.

Chapter Three

Pío Baroja: The Pure Novel

Basque, like Miguel de Unamuno and Ramiro de Maeztu, Pío Baroja
y Nessi is the last of the great novelists belonging to the grand
tradition of the genre, much as Leo Tolstoy (1828–1910), Fyodor
Dostoevski or Charles Dickens (1812–70) were in their time. Generally acknowledged as a direct descendant of Benito Pérez Galdós
and Vicente Blasco Ibáñez, Baroja did little else in his life except
to write novels—two per year in his prime. He held no other
occupation, with the result that his complete works approach the
century mark.[1] Of these, more than half are novels.[2] This writer,
to whom Ernest Hemingway (1898–1961) paid homage as a disciple
on his deathbed,[3] may be considered the greatest novelist not only
of his own Generation of 1898 but, indeed, of the whole of twentieth-century peninsular Spanish literature.

The Life of Pío Baroja

Pío, the youngest of three sons, was born in the Basque city of
San Sebastián on 28 December, 1872. The family's comfortable
middle-class existence, afforded by his father Serafín Baroja's profession as a mining engineer, changed locations several times during
young Pío's early years. The constant moving from city to city (San
Sebastián to Madrid in 1879, Madrid to Pamplona in 1881, back
to Madrid in 1886, to Valencia in 1891, permanently back to
Madrid in 1893) was traumatic enough to prompt Baroja to recall
in later years that his childhood had been an unhappy one.

Neither his secondary nor his university education seems to have
had much of an impact on Baroja, who admitted in his *Memorias*
(Memoirs) to having been a mediocre student.[4] He was disenchanted
with most of his teachers throughout his career, a contempt that
shows clearly in the initial chapters of his 1911 masterpiece novel
El árbol de la ciencia (The Tree of Knowledge) and which almost caused
him to fail his third year medical school examinations at the University of Madrid. The move to Valencia in 1891, then, appears to

have been a propitious change since Baroja successfully completed his studies at the university there. In October 1893 he finished his thesis, "El dolor: Estudio psicofísico" (Pain: a psychophysical study) and received his medical doctor's diploma. Having recently lost his oldest brother Darío from an illness, Baroja wanted to get away from the family home, so he took a job as a country doctor in the small Basque town of Cestona in August 1894. Alone there, he found unwanted competition from another established physician, hostility and ignorance from the villagers, and a decided lack of vocation on his own part to endure a life of service to others and many discomforts to himself. Baroja resigned at the end of thirteen months and returned to Madrid where, together with his brother Ricardo, he took over the running of his aunt Juana's bakery. This business venture turned out to be no more successful than his previous foray into medicine, but it did not matter much; for by the time their bakery went bankrupt, Baroja had begun writing and publishing on a regular basis in several Madrid newspapers and magazines.[5]

Though by no means rich from his articles and short stories, Baroja saw that he could live modestly from his writings and thus he decided to make a career out of it. His parents had bought a two-story house, number 34 Mendizábal Street, and there the whole family lived until the Spanish Civil War in 1936, including his brother Ricardo's wife and his sister Carmen's husband Caro Raggio, who would become Pío's publisher. In time a third floor was added onto the house where the novelist lived with his parents. His father died in 1912, but his mother lived until 1935 when Baroja was in his sixties.

Baroja never married because he never needed a woman to look after him. Basically a shy man, his mother, sister, sister-in-law, and a servant made things easy for him. It is not even certain that he ever had a serious love affair. The life of a bachelor suited him admirably. Baroja was free to do as he pleased when he pleased, though it appears that his worst vice, if it can be labeled thus, was traveling. Like his fellow "ninety-eighters," Baroja journeyed throughout all of Spain by coach, train, and often on foot. Many of his novels, especially the early ones, such as *Camino de perfección* (The righteous path, 1902) and *Zalacaín el aventurero* (Zalacaín the adventurer, 1909), recount in artistic form these wanderings. He also traveled to many countries in Europe. To Paris he went no less than a dozen times; he also visited London, Switzerland, Germany, Denmark, Belgium, and Holland, and particularly liked Rome, Florence, and Milan in Italy.

In 1900, the year he made the first of his trips to the French capital, Baroja's life as a novelist began in earnest. His first books *Vidas sombrías* (Somber lives) and *La casa de Aizgorri* (The House of Aizgorri) appeared in print then, although Baroja had to underwrite the costs of the publication himself and the works sold less than a couple of hundred copies. No matter, critical reaction was favorable, and he was determined to make a go of it. Baroja's life was one of habits that changed little, save for the forced three-year hiatus (1936–39) of the Spanish Civil War, until he died two months before his eighty-fourth birthday. He customarily rose at eight in the morning and sat down to write at nine, a task that lasted until lunchtime at one o'clock. The midday meal was followed in later years by a nap and then a walk, usually alone, through the neighborhood and Alcalá Street (a main thoroughfare), which included visits to secondhand bookstores or to the newsroom of some daily to pass the time and see acquaintances. Baroja normally had dinner early and then went to bed where he read until well past midnight. Such was the routine, tranquil life of the man whose characters are notorious adventurers and daring men of action.

In 1912, seeking to regain some of his Basque heritage so distant in Madrid, Baroja bought the old manorial house of Iztea in Vera del Bidasoa, northern Spain, that—once restored—became his favorite residence. He moved there all of his books and paintings given to him by the contemporary artists Darío de Regoyos (1857–1913) and his brother Ricardo, and there spent the better part of the year. As soon as he had finished his book and turned the manuscript over to his publisher in the early spring, Baroja would journey north to Iztea and there remain until late autumn, bringing a new novel back with him to Madrid to Caro Raggio. In 1912, the year *El mundo es ansí* (The way of the world) was published, his father died and his younger sister Carmen married.

The years went by uneventfully, Baroja never deviating from his bourgeoislike habits, his fame increasing noticeably to the point where his novel *Zalacaín el aventurero* was made into a film "with Baroja himself in one of the minor roles."[6] In 1934 he was selected as a member of Spain's most prestigious and exclusive literary association, the Royal Academy of Letters. The following year, on the afternoon of 12 May, he read his entrance speech, "La formación psicológica de un escritor" (The psychological makeup of a writer). His mother died at that time. One year later while in his summer house at Vera, Baroja had an unpleasant and—he felt—dangerous encounter with a regiment of soldiers, which prompted him to flee, on foot, his country's civil war. He remained in France until 1940, having unsuccessfully attempted a trip to South America earlier that year, when he returned to Spain.

The Barojas had lost everything during the strife. Don Pío, in his seventies and past his creative zenith, saw himself forced to write once again in order to survive economically. Thus, fighting an incipient cerebral arteriosclerosis, the old man began putting together his *Memorias* and a last handful of novels. A new edition of his complete works was savagely cut by the Franco censorship. Trials such as these, together with the deaths of Ricardo and Carmen, probably made the last years of Baroja's life unhappy. Only the company of his nephew, the anthropologist Julio Caro, and the presence of younger novelists such as Camilo José Cela (1916–) and José Luis Castillo Puche (1919–) enlivened his waning years in the daily *tertulias* at his new apartment on Ruiz de Alarcón Street near Retiro Park. He died on 30 October, 1956 and was buried the following day in Madrid's civil cemetery.

Ideology, Style, and Structure of Baroja's Novels

If Baroja was successful as a novelist, not only from literature's lasting vantage point but even in his own time, it is because he discovered very early in his writing career an approach to fiction so perfectly suited to his ideas about life and literature that he never needed to agonize over literary creation once he had written his first best-seller, *Camino de pefección,* in 1902. After this novel—his third— Baroja wrote steadily for half a century, unconcerned with method, aesthetics, or theories regarding the novel. Years later, looking back in 1947 in his memoirs *Galería de tipos de la época* (Portrait gallery of contemporaries), Baroja confessed that he had always been the same, that his ways at the age of twenty remained unchanged when he was past sixty: "I have not found anything in my existence to make me change my mind ever."[7]

The uncomplicated existence of this "humble wanderer," as Baroja liked to refer to himself, runs a parallel course in his literary production. Baroja disliked innovation of any type, at least the conscious or artificial kind. He wrote to earn a little money, he said, and to keep himself entertained.[8] His greatest fear when writing was the possibility of boring his readers; consequently his narratives all strive to tell a story in engaging fashion. He uses a style that communicates in plain language, giving his short paragraphs a directness and clarity that reflect an aversion to words he had not heard or were not used around the house by his parents or someone in his family.

The sole impediment to a total enjoyment of Baroja's works by a mass readership can probably be blamed on the undying pessimism that clouds all of his writings. By temperament Baroja was a skeptic with little faith in man's innate goodness or in society's ruling principles. Even though his closest friends referred to him as a gentle and unassuming individual, those who knew him less well, either as casual acquaintances or in professional dealings, invariably characterized him as unsociable, gruff, and unapproachable. Significantly, no one ever referred to Baroja as a friendly, cheerful, or even a considerate man. His hospital training and later his practice as a physician, both depressing and unrewarding experiences, further contributed to convince Baroja of life's unrelenting misery and lack of lasting happiness. A voracious reader, Baroja during his youth and through his adulthood pored over social and philosophical treatises that by his own admission he probably did not fully understand. The English philosopher Thomas Hobbes (1588–1679) and the Germans Immanuel Kant (1724–1804), Arthur Schopenhauer (1788–1860), and Friedrich Nietzsche (1844–1900) all left an impression on him, easily traceable throughout most of his works. Fueled by these readings, Baroja's lack of faith in God or in a religion of any sort, his mistrust of society and government, and his conviction that man was innately evil color his fiction in dark, pessimistic, and often bitter tones.[9] At times anarchistic, at others nihilistic, always agnostic, the totality of Baroja's production is a catalog of human flaws and life's pitfalls.

And yet, in spite of his varying philosophical notions of doom, Baroja managed to make his fiction entertaining, popular, and lasting. He accomplished this difficult feat time and again by his unequaled ability as a great storyteller. His protagonists are all sincere, iconoclastic individuals whose idealism is invariably neutralized by their inability to act in defense of their beliefs. Society is indifferent to their plight or else life in its fatalistic dimension manages to snuff them out. The settings are by and large urban, either recognizable sites such as Madrid and its lower-class outskirts, or travelogues through the Castilian or Basque regions. This technique of focusing on detailed, known locations probably held a great deal of appeal for his readers who could easily identify them. The plots develop rapidly and in straightforward fashion; several events seldom take place at the same time in Baroja's fiction, unlike Valle Inclán's or Pérez de Ayala's late novels. Action centers almost exclusively on the protagonist; rarely does anything happen when he or she is not present.

The narrative structure is very much open-ended, a characteristic that can arguably be ascribed to Baroja's lack of a premeditated or fully developed outline: "I write my novels without a plan. . . . I need to write paying attention to details."[10] This loose-ends plot yields a porous format where characters appear, disappear, and reappear sometimes in the same work, sometimes years later in other works as secondary figures or protagonists. Much as in real life, Baroja's slices of life show an incompleteness and lack of total meaning that is both disturbing and appealing in its familiarity. The struggle for life—an expression that serves as the title for one of his best-known trilogies—is his most constant theme and the one with which his readers can identify best. In spite of his pessimism and of his indefensible—though not humorless—anti-Semitic and antifeminist attitudes, Baroja has remained as much a favorite of readers as of scholars. However oblivious he may have professed to be to the two camps, Baroja has been well treated by both. In his lifetime, the sales of his books allowed him to live with few economic worries, and the way he wrote them elicited the most renowned treatise on the genre in Spanish from the pen of the philosopher José Ortega y Gasset, *Ideas sobre la novela (Thoughts on the Novel)* in 1925.

Nature and Classification of Baroja's Novelistic Output

Aside from one book of poems, *Canciones del suburbio* (Songs of the outskirts, 1944), memoirs, biographies, and collected essays, Baroja wrote a total of sixty-seven novels between 1900 and 1953, dates of publication of *La casa de Aizgorri* and *Los amores de Antonio y Cristina* (The loves of Antonio and Cristina). Initially Baroja began publishing his novels as separate works without paying much attention to how they related to one another in a larger context. Then, as he began returning to certain themes or characters, it occurred to him that he could group most of them into divisions to facilitate matters for his readers and for himself. He put into practice this idea when writing *La busca (The Quest)* in 1904, a novel so long that no publisher would take it until Baroja divided it into three books, the other two being *Mala hierba (Weeds),* also issued in 1904, and *Aurora roja (Red Dawn)* which appeared the following year. He subtitled the ensemble "La lucha por la vida" (The struggle for life). Thereafter, some times with more justification than others, and even retrospectively, Baroja grouped his novels—except for perhaps a dozen—into trilogies, a classification that, though at times inexact, has been accepted by critics and readers alike as a reasonable way to organize such a prolific output. While Baroja wrote novels well into his eighties, as the dates of *Las veladas del Chalet Gris* (Evenings in the Hotel Gris, 1952), and *Los amores de Antonio y Cristina* attest, his best work ends in 1936 with *El cura de Monleón* (The priest of Monleón). Indeed, many critics agree that Baroja's freshest, most innovative, and vigorous work was over by 1913, the year wherein concurrently with his novelistic chores he began writing the twenty-two volumes of the *Memorias de un hombre de acción* (Memoirs of a man of action).[11] Little that is new appeared thereafter.

Because of constrictions of space it would be impossible and often unprofitable, due to unevenness of merit, to discuss all of Baroja's novels. What follows is a listing of his best-rated trilogies and a subsequent discussion of a select number of works that in the general critical consensus are representative of Baroja's novel overall. The nine trilogies, two of which contain four instead of three novels, are in chronological order: (1) "Tierra vasca": *La casa de Aizgorri* (1900), *El mayorazgo de Labraz* (1903), *Zalacaín el aventuro* (1909), and *La leyenda de Jaun de Alzate* (1922). (2) "La vida fantástica": *Aventuras, inventos y mixtificaciones de Silvestre Paradox* (1901), *Camino de perfección* (1902), and *Paradox, rey* (1906). (3) "La lucha por la vida": *La busca* (1904), *Mala hierba* (1904), and *Aurora roja* (1905). (4) "El pasado": *La feria de los discretos* (1905), *Los últimos románticos* (1906), and *Las tragedias grotescas* (1907). (5) "La raza": *La dama errante* (1908), *La ciudad de la niebla* (1909), and *El árbol de la ciencia.*

(6) "El mar": *Las inquietudes de Shanti Andía* (1911), *El laberinto de las sirenas* (1923), *Pilotos del altura* (1929), and *La estrella de Capitán Chimista* (1930). (7) "Agonías de nuestro tiempo": *El gran torbellino del mundo* (1926), *Las veleidades de la fortuna* (1927), and *Los amores tardíos* (1927). (8) "La selva oscura": *La familia de Errotacho* (1931), *El cabo de las tormentas* (1932), and *Los visionarios* (1932). (9) "La juventud perdida": *Las noches del Buen Retiro* (1934), *El cura de Monleón* (1936), and *Locuras de carnaval* (1937).

The Basque First Steps

A few months after the appearance in 1900 of the thirty-five short stories written between 1892 and 1899, and gathered in the volume entitled *Vidas sombrías,* Baroja published his first novel, *La casa de Aizgorri.* Chronologically the inaugural work in the trilogy "The Basque Country," this novel was conceived initially as a dramatic piece and written in its entirety in dialogue form with a few asides and descriptive or situational annotations.

Being a first novel, in many ways it is atypical. Its dialogued structure appears only two more times in all of Baroja's production, in the fourth volume of this initial series, *La leyenda de Jaun de Alzate* (The legend of Jaun de Alzate), and in *Paradox, rey (Paradox, King),* which belongs to the second trilogy called "The Fantastic Life." *La casa de Aizgorri*'s positive love ending is an infrequent occurrence in Baroja's fiction. Only in "The Struggle for Life" do we find another instance of a happy couple at the conclusion of a trilogy. And finally *La casa de Aizgorri* lacks the censorious tone with which Baroja typically addresses the middle-class bourgeoisie in the bulk of his later works.

Recognizably Barojian, however, is this novel's fast-paced plot, entirely contained in the dialogue. Reminiscent of the nineteenth century's social realism, *La casa de Aizgorri* pits an industrious liberal element (represented by a generation of young aristocrats and professionals supported by the old noble caste who are fighting for progress and some sort of social justice) against an entrenched, devious group of foreign profiteers, anarchists, and striking workers. These characters also foreshadow Baroja's later personages in the directness of their speech, the strength of their convictions, and their readily identifiable goodness or evilness. The narrative structure likewise reminds the reader of Baroja's preference for an open-ended fictional account where characters come and go and incidents can be added or deleted, allowing for change but without detriment to the organic nature of the work.

In addition to those elements that may be more or less characteristically Barojian, *La casa de Aizgorri* possesses certain unique features that make it notable. Foremost among them are the theses of renovation, progress, and the lessening of human suffering. Hastily and perhaps even a bit single-mindedly, Agueda Aizgorri, aided by her resourceful suitor Mariano Unzueta, attempts to turn her father's poisonous (in the economic, medical, moral, and even ecological senses) liquor distillery into a hospital. In order to prevail they must overcome the sabotaging tactics of the distillery's foreman who is also in love with Agueda, her father's alcoholic inertia, and her brother's lack of willpower. Mariano and Agueda's triumph is manifold, resulting in their union as lovers, in the discontinuance of the distillery's pernicious influence as it burns down to make room for the promised hospital, and in the infusion of new life into the bloodline of the old and declining but noble Aizgorri family line with Mariano's industrial and professional resources.

The symbolism in *La casa de Aizgorri* is no less transparent than its good versus evil character plot, but no less engaging either. The Aizgorri family dog, Erbi, growls at Díaz, the treacherous foreman, and at Alfort, the French profiteer, but licks the hand of Mariano or wags its tail at Julián, the family doctor. When a character speaks Castilian, his accent will remain recognizably Basque if he is allied to the good cause, or be mistaken for an ordinary Spaniard if his allegiance is suspect. *La casa de Aizgorri,* though lacking in greatness, represents an admirable first effort by a young novelist—Baroja was twenty-eight at the time of its publication. Its nineteenth-century ascendancy shows, but equally recognizable are some fundamentally Barojian future traits.

The four novels of this series—*La casa de Aizgorri, El mayorazgo de Labraz* (The lord of Labraz), *Zalacaín el aventurero* (Zalacaín the adventurer), and *La leyenda de Jaun de Alzate*—have in common a similar dialogued narrative structure shared by the first and the fourth ones, the Basque settings common to all, and the Basque ancestry of its main characters. In little else do they resemble each other. Given the twenty-odd year lapse that separates the writing of the first from the last, it is not difficult to apprehend the heterogeneity of the foursome or the growing merit accorded especially to *La casa de Aizgorri* and *Zalacaín el aventurero* over the others. The latter work is justifiably celebrated because its background (the Carlist Wars), its structure (the journey), its plot (adventure followed by adventure), and its protagonist (a wandering young noncomformist) all represent what in the minds of many typifies the essential Baroja. It is true: *Aventuras, inventos y mixtificaciones de Silvestre Paradox* (Adventures, inventions and hoaxes of Silvestre Paradox) and *Camino de perfección,* above all, as well as many of Baroja's other novels, combine the same narrative, structural, and character parameters exhibited by *Zalacaín el aventurero.*

The Quest for a More Perfect World

Aventuras, inventos y mixtificaciones de Silvestre Paradox (1901), *Camino de perfección* (1902), and *Paradox, King* (1906) of the series "The Fantastic Life," together with the three novels belonging to "The Struggle for Life," are all read with equal frequency, and both groupings represent Baroja's most successful trilogies.

The three novels belonging to the trilogy "The Fantastic Life" share to some degree in the Generation of 1898's concern for reform in a Spain that—though stagnant—rejected new ideas or methods, in the interest that all of the "ninety-eighters" had in the Spanish landscape, in the journey as a narrative and structural device, and in the reappearance of several of the same characters in all the novels.[12] Silvestre Paradox and Diz de la Iglesia are the main characters in both *Aventuras, inventos y mixtificaciones de Silvestre Paradox* and *Paradox, King;* Fernando Ossorio, the protagonist of *Camino de perfección,* appears briefly with his nymphomaniacal Aunt Laura in the last scenes of the first work of the trilogy.

Aventuras, inventos y mixtificaciones de Silvestre Paradox introduces the character of the same name who wanders through Spain and France frequenting taverns and boardinghouses while accompanied by his sidekick Avelino Diz de la Iglesia. Their lives of travel and constant disorder are filled with numerous meetings with comical, almost caricaturesque, personages. As eccentric as the two are, these encounters in diverse places, which constitute most of the novel, result in chaotic and always humorous incidents. A lack of plot frees Baroja's hand to have these characters roam from place to place following their whims in a search whose motives remain unclear until their story is taken up once again five years later in *Paradox, King.*

By the time this work appeared in print in 1906, Baroja was already thought of as the premier novelist of his generation. He had written seven other novels, among them the early masterpiece *Camino de perfección,* and now the public eagerly awaited the sequel to the earlier popular *Aventuras . . . de Silvestre Paradox. Paradox, King* picks up the thread of Paradox and Diz de la Iglesia's lives in Valencia where they were last seen and resumes the farcical tone of their story. Soon, and for the remainder of the new work, however, the tones become more somber and the tale takes on the characteristics of a black comedy. The initial and most noticeable difference between the two works is the use of dialogue to tell the story. The technique, already used in *La casa de Aizgorri,* contributes greatly to the more accelerated narrative tempo of *Paradox, King.* It is as though Baroja were ridding himself of all encumbrances to facilitate the telling of his heroes' adventures.

Inevitably—even though the novel is divided into chapters—due to the exclusive use of a dialogue format, one tends to regard it almost in terms of acts, a notion that Baroja may have anticipated by splitting it into three parts. Unity of space would seem to dictate and vaguely correspond to the scenarios of the work. The first, which takes place in Spain and Tangiers, reveals Paradox's intent to travel to a remote part of Africa to colonize a nation. The second part follows Paradox and his friends on their maritime voyage as they fight storms and a mutinous crew aboard the "Cornucopia," ending up shipwrecked on the African coast. The last segment focuses on the founding of a new nation where primitive black people and "civilized" white men coexist precariously under the elected monarchical rule of Silvestre Paradox. The utopian enclave comes to an end when a French regiment overruns the settlement and further "civilizes" it by bringing syphilis, alcoholism, gambling, murder, and other telltale advancements of Western European culture. Baroja's bitter and satirical recriminations against society's ills are all too clear in *Paradox, King.* Here they involve not only Spain's but, given the international make up of the cast—English, French, Jewish, Italian, etc.—a universal malaise which he regarded as inescapable. This novel no longer qualifies as one of characters, but is instead a social novel. Its theme can be summed up almost aphoristically by saying that Baroja believes civilization to be the mother of all vices and the father of all ills.

Although the three works of this trilogy are equally celebrated by the reading public, an overwhelming critical consensus has assigned to *Camino de perfección* a superior literary worth, in fact labeling it Baroja's earliest masterpiece and one of the two or three best works to come from his pen. Its title and the subtitle, "Pasión mística" (Mystical passion), taken from Santa Teresa of Avila's homonymous autobiographical work, are nothing but an ironic twist on the reality of the novel and its protagonist, Fernando Ossorio, who forever strays in a fruitless search to find a way of life with a meaning and a purpose. Widely considered a novel of ideas that best voiced what the Generation of 1898 meant to say, *Camino de perfección* may very well be the most representative of the novels to come not only from Baroja but from the rest of his contemporaries as well in its embodiment of all of their social and existential concerns: a cry for reform, a look at the most somber aspects of Spanish life in cities and villages, an accusation of lack of willpower *(abulia)* on the part of Spaniards in all classes, and an admiration for the untainted beauty of the landscape. Diffuse in plot and structure—to a greater extent than any other Baroja novel—*Camino de perfección* follows a narrative format along the footsteps of its protagonist as he walks through Madrid, Colmenar, Manzanares, Segovia, Toledo, and other towns and cities in Castile encountering deviousness, mistrust, and unsociability more frequently than not.[13]

This critical panorama of Spain, a look at its people—where and how they live, what they do, and what they are like—is less a novel than a loosely conceived narrative of philosophical judgments and opinions structured around a protagonist who is not always the most important character in scenes along his treks. At times *Camino de perfección* resembles a travelogue, at others a catalog of faults, and yet at others a gallery of personages of all ilks. For the most part, they are rogues who personify the lack of sociability Baroja felt typifies most Spaniards. Ironically, all the men and women from the upper classes exhibit nothing more comforting than contempt for Ossorio and his guest; only the most humble (a garbage collector) or nonnatives (Max Schultze) show any sympathy for the hero. The character of Fernando Ossorio differs from those of Paradox and Zalacaín, especially the latter, in the voluntary choice of a life of adventure and wandering. The former two had both been obliged to become vagabonds as a result of dire economic straits. Fernando abandons his sedentary life in Madrid only because he feels at a dead end. Troubled by the lack of meaning in his life, he sets out in a search for a better, more peaceful and meaningful existence. His character is nurtured by a strong idealism that blindly tries to find true, absolute, and pure values in human existence. Unable to find them anywhere in Spain or in any of its people, the hero reconciles himself to this earth and looks instead for consolation in his marriage to a simple girl named Dolores (Spanish for "grief" or "pain"), with whom he lives an uncomplicated existence in a small coastal village. Baroja's alternatives become once again clear in the choice that his protagonist has made: to be aware of life's full reality is to suffer and be desolate; if one wishes to survive, it is necessary to anesthetize oneself to those harshest realities and lead the life of a petit bourgeois.

From the Picaresque to the Bourgeois

When Baroja began the serialization of *The Quest* in the Republican newspaper *El Globo* in the year 1903, he realized that the novel was much too long to be issued as a single work. He therefore rewrote *The Quest* as a two-part work and added to it further, necessitating a third volume. Baroja titled the new books *Weeds* and *Red Dawn*. All three were published as separate volumes (in 1904 the first two, and in 1905 the third one) but in a trilogy form entitled "La lucha por la vida" (The struggle for life). In fact, however, from the point of view of structure, plot and characters, *The Quest, Weeds,* and *Red Dawn* are but one work. The three parts may be a typographical or an editorial convenience, but from an intrinsically literary point of view, each represents no more than a stage in the protagonist Manuel Alcázar's life as he grows from destitute orphan, to *pícaro*, to petit bourgeois. This progression serves Baroja to paint a kaleidoscope of contemporary life in Madrid that, though impressionistic, manages to cut a wide swath across all social strata: from prostitutes to prosperous businessmen, from shoemakers to tavern owners, from garbage collectors to sculptors, from boardinghouse dwellers to grand hotel guests, and from thieves to assassins to messianic anarchists. As he had done in the two *Paradox* novels, *Zalacaín* and *Camino de Perfección*, Baroja utilizes his protagonist not only in his role of principal character but also as the center of the plot and the delineator of the narrative. Consequently, the narrative structure is again disperse and nearly plotless, resembling a juxtaposed succession of vignettes or daily occurrences in the life of Manuel and those with whom he comes into contact.

The Quest thematically, structurally, and protagonistically is a typical picaresque novel. Manuel worries about nothing but food and shelter, having to live by his wits. At times he has neither, and his struggle is so difficult that he ends up with nothing more than a meal or a cot. The quest announced in the title symbolizes Manuel's unrewarding job-to-job search for economic, social, and sentimental stability. Instead he reaps a painful, intimate, and lasting knowledge of Madrid's lower working and criminal classes. His "struggle for life" extends to the menial and sometimes unlawful occupations of errand boy, baker's apprentice, photographer, typesetter, junk collector, petty thief, confidence man, and jailbird. The last few of these experiences carry Manuel into *Weeds* where the focuses of his existence gradually expand from the previous preoccupations of food and shelter to the less despairing choice of where to work and in what capacity. The turning point in his aimless existence comes when, caught sleeping with a group of vagrants in the city's outskirts, he halfway understands one policeman say to another: "These [bums] are no longer redeemable."[14] Realizing that all he has to do to fall into a life of misery, poverty, sickness, and early death is to continue as he has been, Manuel—with the providential aid of his friend Roberto Hastings—actively opts for a change. The most telling sign of Manuel's stepping into the establishment side of life is his collaboration with the policeman Ortiz to capture his one-time friend "El Bizco" wanted for yet another murder. There is a final hopeful—though weak and almost dreamlike—note in *Weeds* when Manuel and his friend Jesús contemplate a starry sky while they stroll aimlessly in the suburbs of Madrid, musing aloud about a brighter future. This wistful ending sets the tone for the last installment of "The Struggle for Life."

Red Dawn, a title that both threatens and bodes well, alludes to the promise of a new life, but also warns of the dangers involved in the excesses that anarchy and other revolutionary ideas can wreak upon everyone. Touched by them, Manuel's brother Juan, an ardent and idealistic anarchist, becomes a victim of his own ideological fervor; a similar fate overtakes other friends, among them Jesús. Ironically, the latter's sister, Salvadora, unable to "save" her own brother, manages to intercede on behalf of Manuel's spiritual well-being, thus rescuing him from the dangers that had engulfed the rest. Manuel's marriage to Salvadora and the ownership of a printing shop complete his transformation from a displaced indigent to an established petit bourgeois.

Overly laden with ideological commentary, the narrative structure of *Red Dawn* turns from disperse to discursive. The tempo slows to a crawl when ideology and action are merely discussed and argued about by the proponents and opponents of differing factions. In the end Baroja need not have gone to such lengths, since he implicitly managed to discredit spokesmen of all persuasions (anarchists, socialists, monarchists) through their caricaturesque behavior. Besides, though Baroja—like Manuel—may have seen little harm in talking revolution, he also saw little benefit in participating in it. Manuel's marriage results in relative economic prosperity but intellectual discontent—a balance that probably struck Baroja as the only compromise that life willingly extends to most individuals.

Resignation from Life

Only one gesture binds the three diverse novels in "La raza" (Race), *La dama errante* (The wandering lady, 1908), *La ciudad de la niebla* (The city of fog, 1909), and *El árbol de la ciencia* (The Tree of Knowledge, 1911), into a trilogy—the nexus being that all center on a physician: the first two on the same character named Enrique Aracil, the third on a totally different person, Andrés Hurtado. The tenuous connection between *La dama errante* and *La ciudad de la niebla* is maintained only insofar as both works have as a historical basis the assassination attempt by the anarchist revolutionary Mateo Morral against Spain's King Alfonso XIII on his wedding day, 31 May, 1906.[15] Further similarities are nonexistent both between these two works and also when compared with *The Tree of Knowledge*. The latter truly stands alone, not only in terms of subject matter, structure, and characters, but also by reason of its merit as an autonomous work of art. *The Tree of Knowledge,* Baroja's own favorite novel, was written at the height of his intellectual powers and represents the zenith of the genre as practiced by the Generation of 1898. It is, at the same time, recognizably Barojian, individualistic, and generational. Of undeniable narrative interest, *The Tree of Knowledge* also contains a profoundly philosophical commentary, presented in the long dialogues between Andrés Hurtado and his uncle Dr.

Iturrioz, which is so perfectly integrated into the novel that without it the protagonist's future existence and death would be incomprehensible. *The Tree of Knowledge,* first and foremost, is a novel of character and thesis, which takes philosophy—mostly Schopenhauerian pessimism—to mean not only a manner of thinking, but also a way of acting out—that is, living—these notions. Besides being a work of a truly original nature, it is notable for its autobiographical content, since, although Baroja was similar in personality to many of his protagonists, he came closest in age, temperament, occupation, philosophical outlook, and even place of residence to Andrés Hurtado.[16]

Of generational interest in a critical sense, *The Tree of Knowledge* touches upon nearly all of the dimensions that Unamuno, Valle Inclán, Baroja, Azorín, and Maeztu customarily depicted as lacking in Spanish society. Criticism of life in the big city has as its backdrop Madrid, where Baroja does not neglect any social, economic, or political aspect deserving of a chastising note. On the entertainment scene, he rails against the bloody spectacle of bullfighting where masses are concerned and the casino where the idle and the rich drink, plot, and gamble. Neither institutions nor professions escape Baroja's wrath: universities and professors, hospitals and doctors, the armed forces and military personnel, government and state officials, theaters and dramatists, newspapers and the press corps; all of these and other lesser culprits in Spain's downhill slide toward the morass that had already began to envelop the country come in for repeated and direct criticism. Set precisely in the years contemporary with the Spanish-American War, part 6, "La experiencia en Madrid" (The experience in Madrid), exhibits an unbiased estimation of Spain at the turn of the century through the clinical eyes of Dr. Iturrioz, who (having earlier been in America) forecasts accurately for his nephew Andrés the sure outcome of the uneven conflict between Spain and the United States. In contrast to the doctor's sobering and cynical appraisal, Baroja tells—from Andrés's ingenuous point of view—of the prevailing Spanish attitudes that, fueled by the rhetoric of a bombastic press and an ineffective government, mislead Spaniards into thinking that the United States forces lack the will to fight. The outcome, as predicted by Dr. Iturrioz, reinforces Andrés's admiration of his uncle and makes him the only man from whom Andrés seeks counsel and friendship thereafter.

Completely steeped in this background of generational and historical concerns, man's existential predicament is embodied in the life of Andrés Hurtado. As expected, in Baroja's fiction character dictates narrative structure and *The Tree of Knowledge* is no different. The protagonist's actions, thoughts, and words prescribe the route of the novel; nothing happens without Hurtado around. His outlook on life reflects faithfully the pessimistic ideas of the philosopher Schopenhauer, especially those found in his 1819 treatise *Die Welt als Wille und Vorstellung (The World as Will and Idea)*. Baroja, who owned a copy of it in French and who had read it many times, fictionalized a great many of its contentions in this novel, among them the argument that knowledge meant suffering. E. Inman Fox, quoting, from book 4 of *The World as Will and Idea*, writes: "the more distinctly a man knows, the more intelligent he is, the more pain he has; the man who is gifted with genius suffers most of all."[17]

The central idea around which Baroja erected the narrative and structural framework, as well as the changing character of his protagonist Andrés Hurtado, is the age-old *sic et nunc* (yes and no) debate between action and thought. Andrés, when finally prepared to posit this dilemma on his own—life or reflection?—hears his oracle uncle Iturrioz tell him that only two choices remain open to him. Either he does nothing and adopts an indifferent attitude toward life or he can choose to act but with the following caveat: he must limit the radius of his actions lest he become ineffective in accomplishing them.[18] Andrés, with some exceptions (he marries against his uncle's advice), chooses the second option and begins to act within a well-defined and narrow scope.

Andrés's desired success, which he may have unconsciously targeted as *ataraxia* (a state of peace or contentment without religious or even ethical overtones insofar as the Greeks defined it), does not come about any more than it had up to this decisive moment in his life. Each of the successive stages in Andrés's existence constitutes a failure, from the time he is first seen as a teenager until he takes his own life at the end of the book. As a son he fails in his intolerance of his father's vices and extravagant attitudes, symbolically seeking isolation and refuge from his family in the home's attic. He fails as a student because, though intelligent and caring, he does not apply himself and has to resort to Dr. Iturrioz to intercede with the professors he hates in order to pass his courses. He fails as a practicing physician because, unwilling to compromise his principles, he becomes increasingly unsociable and alienates himself from his patients and colleagues alike. He fails as a husband because he considers love and sex the price that he must pay for the companionship he seeks in the marriage. Ultimately Andrés fails as a man because, though operating within a reduced scope—symbolically, he has ordered most of the walls in their married apartment torn down so that there is one large main room where he works, eats, sleeps, and carries out most of his activities—he cannot either act in his capacity as the healer of others (he is reduced to translating and eventually writing essays for a medical journal) or go on living when his wife and son die at childbirth.

As an admirer of Espronceda,[19] Andrés shared the great romantic poet's vital dilemma: his ideals were out of tune with life's baser reality. Life, for both, could never measure up to what either wanted it to be. This irreconcilable difference led Espronceda to dwell poetically on the only solution—death, or the peace of the sepulcher as he put it.[20] Andrés imitated him, but in a very real sense, by injecting himself with an overdose of a morphine derivative. When life's burden of awareness became too painful for Andrés to bear alone, he simply chose to withdraw from it. He may have been a precursor of a better life as Baroja wrote in the last paragraph, in the sense that he was at least able to achieve an ephemeral *ataraxia*— the very brief weeks of a precariously content marriage.[21]

The End of a Road

The trilogy "Las Ciudades" (The cities) incorporates the most heterogeneous group of Baroja's novels. Only a studied search for links among *César o nada* (*Caesar or Nothing,* 1910), *El mundo es ansí* (The way of the world, 1912), and *La sensualidad pervertida* (*Amorous Experiments of a Simpleminded Man in a Degenerate Age,* 1920) divulges a slight similarity in the misfortunes of each of the protagonists and in the widening span of Baroja's narrative geography. In "The Cities" the fictional horizon shifts from small towns not only to the large Spanish capitals but also to the great cosmopolitan cities of Rome, Florence, Paris, and Geneva. And yet, whether the plot unfolds in a European setting or in a rural Spanish province, Baroja's pessimistic outlook on life remains unchanged. The failed political ambitions depicted in *Caesar or Nothing* are echoed in the personal and sentimental frustrations that Luis Murguía and Sacha Savaroff endure respectively in *Amorous Experiments . . .* and *El mundo es ansí*.

El mundo es ansí is the last of Baroja's narratives to take place in a contemporary setting; henceforth they focus on the past. This novel also concludes his initial period of innovation and growth in the art of storytelling; later works show no new techniques and no significant departures from the writer's methodology, which had matured in the years 1902 to 1912. As if to signal an end to his novelistic experimentation, in 1912 Baroja began to work in earnest on the twenty-two-volume series of the *Memorias de un hombre de acción*.

Referred to by one critic as "his most consistently pessimistic novel,"[22] *El mundo es ansí* offers Baroja's readers a more ample vision, both in terms of characters and locations, than *The Tree of Knowledge*. In this new work the protagonists travel throughout most of the European continent, not just through Spain. Its plot develops almost entirely in a grey and melancholy autumn, consonant with the empty and sad lives of men and women existing on the fringes of communal society, whose destiny alternately showers cruelty, egotism, and harshness upon them. The novel begins in medias res, as the protagonist Sacha, a young Russian divorced from a wretched Swiss Jew, remarries the Spanish painter Juan Velasco, a bon vivant whose only goal is to turn life into a party. The marriage predictably fails. Sacha, once again alone and totally abject, returns to her native country. She realizes in time, however, that her flight to Russia has meant a hurt for someone else in turn, José Ignacio Arcelu, the man who had shown her unrequited love.

A series of repeated sentimental disillusionments, quite similar to the above cited, make up the narrative linear structure of this novel. Its title comes from the legend Sacha found in a coat of arms carved in stone, showing three daggers gripped by as many clenched fists arranged in the shape of a cross and stabbing three hearts. An old stone house in the Basque location of Navaridas where Baroja really did discover the downed coat of arms in 1909, along with his trips to Italy, Switzerland, and France between 1907 and 1909, place author and character much closer to one another than would seem likely at first. Sacha, a medical doctor like the novelist himself, betrays in her hyperaesthetic spirit a kinship to Baroja's own sensibilities. In *El mundo es ansí* it is easy to discern how, in Baroja's eyes, the ways of the world amount to little more than cruelty, grief, and ingratitude. A climate of bitterness and desolation permeates the whole of a work whose title becomes a constant reminder on the lips of Sacha. In a lyrical, melancholy, and disillusioned final paragraph the female protagonist complains: "Yes, everything is violent and cruel in life. So, what to do? One can't stop living, one can't stop, we have to keep going until the very end."[23]

"Such is life," then would seem to be the inescapable concept that Baroja has of society as a whole. And while these may be discouraging words by which to characterize not only *El mundo es ansí,* but the bulk of Baroja's novels, neither their universality nor their timelessness can be appealed. The Irish novelist and playwright Samuel Beckett echoed them a quarter of a century later in *The Unnamable* (1949) in which the final lines read: "Where I am, I don't know, I'll never know, in the silence you don't know, you must go on, I can't go on, I'll go on."[24] Baroja's undeniable pessimism, an even attitude throughout his novelistic production, so clearly voiced in the *homo homini lupus* (man is a wolf to his fellowmen) stance of Dr. Iturrioz in *The Tree of Knowledge,*[25] brings forth a body of fiction with few heroes, and little idealism or drama. For Baroja, life can be endured provided one is lucky. Thus, only a numbered few of his protagonists survive unscathed.

Chapter Four
Ramón del Valle Inclán:
The Aesthetic Novel

Of all the members of the Generation of 1898, Valle Inclán led the most bohemian existence, never settling into a bourgeois routine the way the rest of his contemporaries did. In fact, whereas Unamuno, Baroja, Maeztu, and Azorín all began their mature public lives as nonconformist rebels and slowly changed their attitudes, adopting more moderate stances when fame earned them respectability and financial security, Valle Inclán's trajectory followed the opposite route. His initial position was that of a follower of literary traditions and political conservatism. Only when his genius was recognized did Valle Inclán begin to shed his rightist convictions and adopt an increasing attitude of protest that never waned. The others' metamorphoses followed a predictable pattern from iconoclasm to establishment, while Valle Inclán took exactly the opposite tack. The boast of his most famous character, Xavier de Bradomín, "Spaniards may be divided into two factions: On the one side, the Marqués de Bradomín, and on the other, all the rest,"[1] though clearly a pose, would have pleased Valle Inclán as a characterization of his own stance with regards to his fellow "ninety-eighters."

"Distinguished Poet
and Eccentric Citizen"

The dictator Miguel Primo de Rivera once described Valle Inclán with the phrase "eximio poeta y extravagante ciudadano" (distinguished poet and eccentric citizen), and surely he was not far off. Certainly in contrast with Baroja's routine life, Valle Inclán's was anything but dull. Indeed, it may even be said to rival Blasco Ibáñez's adventurous and novelesque years, though its beginnings were inauspicious enough. He was born on 28 October, 1866 in the small Galician fishing village of Vilanova de Arosa to Ramón Valle, a seaman, and Dolores Peña, who baptized him with the names Ramón José Simón Valle y Peña. The large manorial house where he grew up hints at the noble ancestry on both his father's and his mother's sides, though when the young Ramón tried to lay claim to the titles of Marqués del Valle, Vizconde de Viexín, and Señor del Caramiñal, he was rebuffed by the authorities when he offered no documents as proof.[2] His father had lost a great part of the family's considerable wealth, and he could not be acknowledged as a nobleman so, undaunted, Valle Inclán merely proceeded to change his name to Ramón María del Valle Inclán y Montenegro, something more high-sounding than the one with which he had been christened. In this way he began not only to create literature on paper but to fictionalize his own life. Valle Inclán, mostly referred to by friends and contemporaries as simply Valle, became one of his own interesting characters very early on.

During his high-school years (1877–85) spent in Pontevedra, Valle showed no interest in books and little enthusiasm for playing with others. At the age of nineteen, like most sons of well-to-do middle-class Spanish families, he enrolled as a law student in the nearby University of Santiago de Compostela. There his apathy for studying continued as he spent more time learning Italian and fencing than attending classes. It was then also that he published his first short story, "Babel," in the local magazine *Café con gotas* on 11 November, 1888 and wrote his first poem of thirty-six verses titled "Era el postrer momento" (It was the last moment), which is dated 6 December, 1889.[3] When his father died in the following year, Valle no longer felt compelled to finish his degree, though perhaps financial exigencies may have also influenced his decision to leave the university during the last semester of the program. He went to Madrid and there eked out a meager livelihood by writing articles for liberal newspapers such as *El Globo,* a daily that also reprinted several of his earlier short stories. After a few months with little success, Valle decided to emigrate to Mexico and find his fortune abroad. He arrived in Mexico City in April 1892 and there tried his hand at everything from mercenary soldiering to newspaper reporting without any better luck than he had experienced in the Spanish capital. He managed to publish eight to ten pieces in the Mexican dailies *El Correo Español* and *El Universal,* but, as a soldier, he never rose above the rank of infantryman first class. Less than one year later he left Mexico, stopping off for several weeks at a Cuban plantation, dejected and in such dire straits that the Spanish consul had to pay for his return passage to Spain. Years later these disappointing experiences would be transformed into unqualified successes as they found their way into Valle's literary creations.

Penniless upon his arrival at Pontevedra, Valle must have decided to follow the only constant in his life that up to this point had yielded any promise: writing. Bearded and long-haired, Valle took up marijuana smoking and began attending literary gatherings in the local cafés where he met several influential—though more strait-laced than he—men with university and publishing connections, among them Jesús Murais and Torcuato Ulloa. Their practical advice and wise counsel led Valle to read and write during the years 1893 to 1896 in a more profitable and organized manner than had been his habit up to this time. The most significant outcome of this association and of Valle's frequenting of Murais's private library was the publication of his first book, *Femeninas* (Feminine cameos), in 1895 when the author was twenty-nine years old. Prefaced by the Galician historian, Manuel Murguía, the husband of the poetess Rosalía de Castro and a friend of Valle's father, the slim volume is a collection of six love stories in the manner of the French Parnassians and symbolists.[4] The book met with no success in Pontevedra, where it was published by A. Landín; in Madrid no one knew of it. But back to the capital Valle went in search of his literary fortunes once again, this time protected by a government job provided for him through the offices of his patron Torcuato Ulloa.

Once in Madrid it was not long before Valle lost his taste for bureaucratic chores and voluntarily gave up his sole secure means of support, so that for a while he lived on a small allowance from his family. Valle's needs were few since he made do with a one-room attic apartment on Calvo Asensio Street in a modest neighborhood, eating nothing but *café de recuelo* (coffee perked for a second time over the same grounds, customarily reserved for the poor) and day-old bread (normally half of a small loaf sliced lengthwise, called either *media de arriba* or *media de abajo* depending on whether it was the top or the bottom half) at several of Madrid's literary cafés and taverns where he spent most of his waking hours arguing and telling tall tales. During one of many arguments at the Café de la Montaña, Valle was struck by the newsman Manuel Bueno and his left hand had to be amputated as a cuff link imbedded itself in Valle's wrist and caused an infection. This episode, too, would later be ennobled in its transformation into Valle's literature in the *Sonatas* (1902–5) series.

Outwardly Valle never appeared discouraged by his literary failures. A story, perhaps apocryphal, that has been repeated many times tells of Valle, who, when confronted by someone making light of the fact that only three copies of his early *Femeninas* had sold, picked up a copy of it and tossed it out the window saying that the likeliest reason must have been that the work had not been worth it. He made the best of it, barely earning a living from newspaper collaborations, by performing as an actor or sometimes as a director, and even by writing advertising copy for pharmaceutical products of questionable efficacy. In at least one instance[5] he put into verse a commercial for "plastic flour" to combat indigestion thus:

> En toda fiesta onomástica
> yo os digo:—¡Comed, bebed!
> ¡Atracaos! ¡Absorbed
> la dosis de Harina Plástica!

> (At every saints' day celebrations
> I'm telling you:—Eat! Drink!
> Get bloated! Guzzle
> A dose of Plastic Flour!)

Valle's circle of friends, which included Rubén Darío (1867–1916), Jacinto Benavente (1866–1945), and other well-known figures, decided to produce his play *Cenizas* (Ashes) and use the profits to buy the author an artificial arm. The play premiered on 7 December, 1899 but closed down almost immediately. However, a collection taken up among the cast insured its publication. Another friend from the theater group, the actor Ricardo Calvo, subsidized the publication of Valle's first *Sonata,* the *Sonata de Otoño (Autumn Sonata)* in 1902. The book was an unqualified success and Valle's career as a writer of some importance was launched at last. In the years 1903 to 1905, he wrote three sequels—though some antedate it internally—to the *Autumn Sonata,* corresponding to the other three seasons, which were equally well received. His collaborations were now sought by illustrious journals and newspapers such as *El Imparcial;* he was asked to write introductions to the works of authors already established; his manuscripts were readily accepted by publishers and he even had his own literary clique at the "Café Candelas."

This change in economic fortunes allowed Valle to live in more decorous freedom, and both his health and his appearance took a turn for the better.[6]

In 1907, at the age of forty, Valle fell in love and married the actress Josefina Blanco, who at twenty-seven was one of the best-known leading ladies of the Spanish stage. The marriage, while it produced six children, was not a happy one and the couple lived separately most of their lives. These were difficult times for Valle who, though famous and recognized, could not manage his money, his health, or his family life. For the next five years the writer traveled through Spain, especially in the northern Basque region, in order to document himself for the Carlist War novels he was readying at the time; he staged two more of his plays, *La cabeza del dragón (The Dragon's Head)* and *Cuento de abril* (April story), in 1909 at the Teatro de la Comedia in Madrid, and went on tour with his wife's theater company to South America. In Buenos Aires, literary circles everywhere feted him, and the lectures he was persuaded to give on art, literature, and history were enthusiastically received. Upon their return to Madrid, Valle ran for Parliament *(Cortes)* but lost; however, his prestige was so high at this time that a new magazine, *Nuevo Mundo,* announced with great fanfare—including Valle's photograph—that the Galician author was about to become a regular contributor.

In spite of these and other triumphs (the political setback did not affect him since Valle had always looked upon politics with a jaundiced eye), he decided to move back to Galicia in the fall of 1912. Never very prudent, Valle had let his health deteriorate further, to the point that most photographs of those days show the author in bed, where he did most of his writing. He also felt that while living in the provinces his life as a writer could be easier, both in an economic sense and in terms of the number of hours that—freed of distractions—he could dedicate to his work. As it turns out, Valle did not write very much during the next decade, perhaps because his interest in politics became more serious than heretofore. He ran for Parliament again, several times, but was always defeated, and in 1916 he traveled as war correspondent for *El Imparcial* to the western front in France. He also made frequent trips to Madrid to see his friends, one of whom, the poet Darío, died on 6 February, 1916. These visits encouraged some to think that Valle wanted to return to Madrid, among them the minister of public education, who appointed him professor of aesthetics in the Madrid School of Fine Arts. Valle did not hold the post for even one month, so determined was he to maintain his Galician residency and independence. He did accept eagerly an invitation by President Obregón of Mexico—extended through that country's cultural attaché, the writer Alfonso Reyes—to visit on the nation's centennial anniversary of independence from Spain. The journey, which lasted several months and led him not only to Mexico but to the island of Cuba and the city of New York, must have been a rewarding one for Valle. In sharp contrast to his earlier one, he enjoyed the privileges as a guest of the state and, honored as a literary personage, Valle made the most of his appearances in cafés, literary clubs, and newsrooms. He succeeded in alienating most of the landowners, the vast majority of whom were Spaniards, in both Cuba and Mexico by his reformist statements in press interviews, narrowly avoiding attacks on his person in the two countries. Valle's undiplomatic but honest concern for the underdog in Latin America was to surface unequivocally soon thereafter in his masterpiece novel *Tirano Banderas* (*The Tyrant,* 1926).

Always fearless in his open defiance of governmental authoritarianism and its patent favoritism of the moneyed classes, Valle's increasingly mordant criticism, both in his vocal and in his written diatribes, provoked jail sentences and the heavy hand of the censor. Emblematic of his public stance is his contention, issued on the eve of 1 April, 1922 during a banquet in his honor at the Restaurante Fornos in Madrid, that "the fate of Spanish intellectuals is identical to that of the gypsies: to live persecuted by the *Guardia Civil* (the rural civil guards)."[7] When his play *La hija del capitán* (The captain's daughter), a comical and openly political farce, appeared at Madrid bookstores in 1927, police were dispatched all over the city under government orders to confiscate every copy they could find. Valle, it seems, knew his adversaries well.

By 1930 Valle, having undergone major surgery, had moved back to Madrid and was living comfortably from his earnings as a dramatist and from the sales of his books. He wrote less and less for newspapers since he felt that his writing of fiction would suffer as a consequence, though truly Valle had ended his creative period by this time. His last important novels, *La corte de los milagros* (The court of miracles) and *Viva mi dueño* (Hoorah for my owner), appeared in 1927 and 1928 respectively. Two years later the publication of the three miniplays *Martes de Carnaval* (Shrove Tuesday) marked the end of Valle's career as a serious writer.

Valle's fortunes declined rapidly after 1932, the year in which he finally divorced his wife, Josefina. It was also then that his publisher, C.I.A.P. (Compañía Ibero-Americana de Publicaciones), filed for bankruptcy, leaving the aging writer without economic support. Between hospital stays and further operations attempting to stave off the ravages of cancer, Valle was forced to write again for periodicals of every sort, a task that he loathed for taking so much time and energy from serious writing when he had so little left of either. Mercifully, in 1933 the Republican government named him director of the Spanish Academy of Fine Arts in Rome to ease some of his financial difficulties, but Valle's health was so poor that his stay in Italy lasted only a few months. He returned to Santiago de Compostela, in his native Galicia, in the spring of 1935 and there spent his last days, heroically, between the café *tertulias* and the hospital of his friend and physician, Dr. Villar Iglesias. He died on 6 January, 1936, the year of the outbreak of the Spanish Civil War and also the year that saw the deaths of his friends Miguel de Unamuno, Ramiro de Maeztu, and Federico García Lorca.

Two Aesthetics:
Modernismo and Esperpentismo

For a time Valle was regarded merely as the author of the *Sonatas,* the four miniature novels written in the modernist vein expounded by the Nicaraguan poet Rubén Darío. Thus, Valle was referred to as the modernist member of the Generation of 1898 and considered an artist more preoccupied with aesthetics than with ethics. While this may be an approximate appraisal of the first twelve to fifteen years of his writings, critics and public alike eventually began to realize that Valle was a more complex and committed author than once thought. The *Sonatas* are simply the highest example of Valle's recognizable first stage as a writer.

Félix Rubén García y Sarmiento, better known as Rubén Darío (his familial nickname), together with the Latin American poets José Enrique Rodó (1871–1917), Amado Nervo (1870–1919), José Santos Chocano (1875–1934), and Leopoldo Lugones (1874–1933), extricated Spanish poetry from the postromantic pedestrian verses of Ramón de Campoamor (1817–1901) and Gaspar Núñez de Arce

(1834–1903). These two, among others, inherited the prosaic notions of a warmed-over romanticism and were content with the prosaic themes of home life, transportation, (e.g., Campoamor's famous "El tren expreso" [The express train]), and other lesser muses. Darío's 1888 volume of verses, *Azul* (Blue), took all of Hispanic poetry by storm by virtue of the exoticism of its themes, the newness of its metrics, and the freshness of its language. Spain's most perceptive critic of the time, Juan Valera (1824–1905), today best known for his novels, praised *Azul* and wrote about it with rare admiration. Into *Azul* Darío had assimilated the lyrical aesthetics of the French Parnassian and symbolist authors Pierre Charles Baudelaire (1821–67), Théophile Gautier (1811–72), and Jean Arthur Rimbaud (1854–91) and the Italian Gabriele D'Annunzio (1863–1938), whose world was built on a refined language replete with archaic and arcane terms, on themes of erotic and exotic love affairs, and inhabited by young, sad, and beautiful princesses who kept the company of swans. For Spanish readers it was a welcome relief from the sing-song consonantal rhymes of Campoamor and Núñez de Arce, whom they quickly put aside and easily forgot.

When Darío visited Spain for the second time in 1898, he had already made converts, some of them faithful until their deaths: Francisco Villaespesa (1877–1936); Manuel Machado (1874–1947); the 1957 Nobel Prize winner for literature, Juan Ramón Jiménez (1881–1958); and Ramón Goy de Silva (1888–1962). Valle, too, had fallen under Darío's spell and remained both a disciple and a friend until the latter's death from alcoholism at the age of forty-nine. Valle was drawn to Darío's exquisite microcosm of archaic, refined, and escapist compositions. And he emulated the Nicaraguan's aesthetics of beauty by creating a literature on literature that extended for a decade and a half, a period that began with his first book, *Femeninas* (1895), included the famous *Sonatas,* and ended with the *Comedias bárbaras* (The vandals), written from 1907 to 1923. In this first period, Valle created an imaginary world of gardens and manor houses, arrogant men and nostalgic women, with many lost causes worth fighting for. Slowly, however, this unreal world began to unravel as some of the characters revealed an ugly side dissonant from the rest of the modernist diorama. Valle was outgrowing the aesthetic of "art for art's sake" and turning to a reformist writing more consonant with his beliefs as a citizen who, once an inchoate Carlist sympathizer, now willingly risked imprisonment for his socialist ideals.

Borrowing from the Golden Age poet Francisco de Quevedo (1580–1645) on the one hand and from the painter Francisco de Goya (1746–1828) on the other (two geniuses in the art of satire and the grotesque), Valle invented for himself a new aesthetics of reform and criticism, which he called *esperpento*. The *esperpento* (a frightful or absurd creature) signifies a 180-degree turn in Valle's aesthetics. True, it was an evolution since those works of his middle years, the novels of the Carlist Wars and *Comedias bárbaras* dramas, slowly incorporate more and more deformed or grotesque characters whose voices and actions are a call to truth and reform. From the impressionist and aristocratic literature of the *Sonatas*, Valle's art terminates in a more humanistic and transcendent literature, which, though closer to reality, is no less artistic or appealing. Almost expressionist in its manifestation, the *esperpento* is formally defined in *Luces de Bohemia (Lights of Bohemia)*, Valle's 1924 tragicomedy where Rubén Darío and Bradomín, his heroes of old (reality and fiction), parody *Hamlet's* graveyard scene in a meditation on death that pointedly alludes to their own aesthetic demise. Here, in front of one concave and one convex mirror found in the *Callejón del gato* (The alley of the cat), the classic heroes, visually deformed, turn into *esperpentos*. Henceforth, Valle's literary reality is continually distorted in similar fashion. Disillusionment, sarcasm, exaggeration, caricature, and parody all consort to bring about a literature of black humor; painful, truthful, and constructive in its unrelenting, mordant criticism. It is under the sign of this new aesthetic that Valle begins to write in the second and final stage of his production. To this period belong, together with the inaugural *Lights of Bohemia* and the earlier *Divinas palabras* (Divine words, 1920), the later plays gathered in the 1930 book *Martes de Carnaval*,[9] and his last novels including the masterpiece *The Tyrant*.

The Memoirs of the Marqués de Bradomín

"The Memoirs of the Marqués de Bradomín," as Valle subtitled his *Sonatas*, portraying an admirable don Juan who was "ugly, Catholic and sentimental,"[10] are set during life's four seasons corresponding to the seasonal scheme of the four *Sonatas*. Written in the years 1902 to 1905, they remain Valle's most widely read and best-known works. And though they may be only one aspect of his production, they are a very important one. The writing in the *Sonatas* amounts to the best modernist prose in peninsular Spanish literature. Years later in his 1912 verse drama *La Marquesa Rosalinda* (Lady Rosalind), Valle's poetry reaches similar heights. The artistic perfection of the *Sonatas* amazes even the contemporary reader. Their carefully crafted narrative structures resemble precious mosaics where each individual, brief chapter (there are no formal divisions) becomes a unique and almost autonomous canvas. This fragmentation of short chapters and clipped paragraphs does not detract from the fictional artistry of interest of the works, but does take away from the narrative continuity typically found in the novels of the period.

The integrating force not only of each individual *Sonata* but of the four as a cycle is Xavier, the Marqués de Bradomín. An aging Don Juan who sentimentally does not belong even to his own century—the *Sonatas* are vaguely thought to take place in the nineteenth century—he is truly an angel of deceit. Bradomín turns drab reality into legend by means of artistic and beautiful lies. He transforms everything with aristocratic eyes, preferring not to look upon reality face to face. This slighting of reality blurs away its most disagreeable aspects. The poor servants—more like feudal serfs—become shadows that whisper in their masters' presence, often moving as though they were ballet figures.

Due to Bradomín's dual role—alas, almost a triple one since, as the selector of his own memoirs (*memorias amables,* meaning "good remembrances," and, thus, not *all* of them) he has functioned also as an editor—as narrator and protagonist, there has always been the temptation to identify the author with his first-person narrator. However, although there is little doubt that much in the *Sonatas* may be considered autobiographical—the Galician manor houses as well as the Mexican settings so familiar to Valle, the titled nobility to which he himself aspired, the sympathetic attitude toward the Carlist cause, the amputation of Bradomín's left arm—it must be remembered that Valle was in his mid-thirties when these novels were written, an age far younger than that of the white-haired dandy.

The themes of the *Sonatas* continue to reflect their "art for art's sake" nature in a glaring lack of the struggle for life so prevalent in Baroja's works. Omnipresent death, love as a catalyst, religion as a source of devotion as well as superstition, and tradition as a privilege for aristocracy are the principal themes of the *Sonatas* which further subdivide into various others, befitting the season in question. The *Sonatas* were not written in chronological order, doubtlessly because their author did not foresee a series and did not have the rest of them in mind when he published the *Autumn Sonata* in 1902. Its large critical and financial success, however, prompted Valle to write the other three at the rate of one per year: *Sonata de Estío* (*Summer Sonata,* 1903), *Sonata de Primavera* (*Spring Sonata,* 1904), and *Sonata de Invierno* (*Winter Sonata,* 1905).

The *Spring Sonata,* though it initiates the cycle chronologically as its title would suggest, was the third published in the series. For various reasons it is the least satisfying of the four. Written to fit a posteriori (retrospectively) into an already established pattern, the *Spring Sonata* appears disconnected and at times awkward in its unfolding. Its protagonist is a Bradomín totally lacking in charm, a seducer who behaves like a scoundrel. His petulant attitude suits him well as a twenty year old, but the reader can not sympathize with him for he has no positive virtue other than his title of nobleman and his position as a Vatican guardsman. The foreign setting also does not ring true. Valle, who had not yet visited any of the Italian cities mentioned in the *Spring Sonata,* labors to produce sites and scenes that come off as being too artificial to be believed. This became a self-acknowledged shortcoming a few years later when the author felt a need to travel to the Basque provinces in order to steep himself in the countrysides where the Carlist War he was to write about had taken place.

The formula for the *Spring Sonata* faithfully follows those of the other three works. Bradomín comes to an ancient palace occupied by several pale, pious, and passionate women of differing ages who are vaguely related to him. As well as their paladin, he becomes their seducer. In the case of the *Spring Sonata,* however, things do not go according to plan because of Bradomín's lack of expertise, brashness of character, his target María Rosario's obstinate determination to profess as a nun, and her mother's cold but correct gauging of Bradomín's intentions. Two deaths punctuate the story: one, that of Monsignor Gaetani, which spoils the atmosphere for any of Bradomín's attempts at seduction, and the second, which takes place accidentally as the dandy makes his most daring assault on María Rosario's virtue. At this final death, involving a small child, Bradomín is forced to flee the palace, thwarted for once.

The *Summer Sonata,* set in Mexico and exuding all of the vigors of manhood—passion, cruelty, and impetuousness—is a delight for the senses. In it, though Bradomín remains young, he is now experienced in the ways of the world and confident to the point of self-parody. Defiant, elitist, and disdainful, the protagonist desires only to set himself apart from other men[11] and to be faithful exclusively to his motto, "Despise others and hate oneself."[12] Touches of Oscar Wilde ("Women need only to forget their scruples in order to be happy"),[13] allusions to the Greek Goddess Thaïs, and the French courtesan Ninon du Clos create an ambience of rarefied pleasures further exacerbated by sensory descriptions of the tropical climate of the Mexican regions where the action takes place.

Bradomín sails for the New World on a British frigate, seeking to forget an unhappy love affair. Fortunately, on board he meets an Indian princess, Niña Chole, beautiful and primitive, who soon dispels his gloominess. She becomes a powerful character who overshadows all others in the *Sonatas,* except perhaps Concha of the *Autumn Sonata,* rivaling Bradomín himself. Niña Chole's interest stems from a strong and distinct characterization. Aside from her physical appeal and noble ancestry, Valle endows her with a memorable personality that renders her quite believable. Her heartlessness brings about the death of more than one man, her intelligence allows her to pass for Bradomín's wife, her loyalty to him impels her to forsake her father, her sensuousness permits her to enjoy all of the carnal pleasures that he seeks, and her station as a pagan priestess forces her to be as sacrilegious as Bradomín.

Nearly as important as the characters of Niña Chole and Bradomín is the setting. As stated previously, Valle had visited Mexico in 1892 and thus had some firsthand knowledge of the country; but the lands he portrayed in *Summer Sonata,* though verisimilar, are likely much more exotic than the real thing, in the same sense that the events recounted turn out to be largely anachronistic. Bathed in the constant heat, humidity, and blinding sunlight so stereotypically tropical, Valle's Mexican scenery intoxicates character and reader alike. These are impressionist portraits of shimmering waters, naked savages, and parched soil. This climate, so opposite to that of Valle's Galicia observed in *Autumn Sonata,* at times disturbs the characters to such an extent that their failings seem endless and increasingly graver: cowardice, idolatry, avarice, hatred, and sadism. At others, the heat acts upon them as an aphrodisiac, rendering the most varied eroticisms: nymphomania, incest, homosexuality, and masochism. The *Summer Sonata*, which like the *Spring Sonata* had started out as a short story years earlier,[14] succeeds where the first one failed because of its stronger characterization and its more believable character motivation, as well as its creation of an atmosphere combining landscape and seascape with a sensual and emotional state ideally suited to the theme and the season alluded.

The *Autumn Sonata* is the prototype of all the *Sonatas* and arguably the best of the lot. Its writing suggests a slow elaboration where each word is carefully weighed before finally being chosen; equal care shows in the syntax and in the length and makeup of individual paragraphs. This same slow, deliberate pace typifies the narrative tempo: relaxed, as befits the season, and the age of its protagonist. It is as though everything fit perfectly and harmoniously with every other piece of the work, so great is Valle's craft in this *Sonata*.

The time is melancholy September; the protagonist, an aging dandy; the theme, a long-forgotten love; the setting, an ancestral manor house. There is little action in the *Autumn Sonata;* in its stead, the reader finds conversation, remembrances, and descriptions ranging from the nostalgic (the *ubi sunt?* topos of "where has it all gone?") to the sensuous (the *algolagnia* leitmotiv of sex and suffering). Back in his native Galicia at the family's eighteenth-century palace of Brandeso, the aging Marqués de Bradomín—last scion of his lineage—receives a letter from a woman loved years ago who beckons him to her death bed. Her name is Concha (María de la Concepción),[15] his thirty-one-year-old cousin who—though since married—still loves Xavier and wishes to see him one last time.

The days spent together by the former lovers—almost the entirety of the novel—illuminate Bradomín's character at its sharpest. He becomes not only the lover of old, forcing Concha to postpone her inclination to repent, but also the cynical and disingenuous dandy, more interested in appearances and effects than in a commitment of substance. Once again he becomes the cynic for whom everything useful is ugly. He prefers to shock Concha with his blasphemies and sacrilegious conduct rather than allow her a devout preparation for death. Bradomín's penchant for the morbid and the perverse causes him to find her more sexually attractive the more ill she turns. Concha becomes a goddess for his pleasures, suffering while Bradomín amuses himself. Yet, in spite of the hero's insincere posturing, Bradomín is not an altogether disagreeable protagonist: a connoisseur of literature and the arts, he has wealth which allows him to be generous and contemplative—if arrogant and self-indulgent in the meanwhile—and the sentimentality that draws him to beautiful women and hopeless causes.

Equally important, once again, is the setting of this *Sonata,* a millenarian Galicia whose feudal past does not seem at all remote. A cold climate of fog and drizzle envelops these aristocratic and refined personages in settings far removed from workaday reality. Their world includes not only the ancient manor houses with chapels and servants' quarters but also the neglected eighteenth-century gardens frequented by pages who care for falcons and horses, the vineyards that are part of the estate, and the yearly tribute paid them by those who work their lands. All of these traditions conjure up an old and lingering past set in the green and humid Galician country, making *Autumn Sonata* more a novel of mood or situation than of character, unique in capturing artistically an age and a region. Perhaps conscious of this achievement, Valle used many of its characters (not only Bradomín but Don Juan Manuel Montenegro and others) and its settings in later works—in the *Sonatas* of course, but also in some of the Carlist War novels, in several plays, and even in the poems of *Aromas de leyenda* (The aromas of a legend) and *El pasajero* (The passenger)[16]—without, however, reaching the pinnacle that the *Autumn Sonata* represents.

The *Winter Sonata,* the last *Sonata* written and the final chapter as well in Bradomín's memoirs, takes place in the Basque provinces where the Carlist Wars were waged throughout the nineteenth century. It concerns the last years of the aged Marqués as he seeks to serve the pretender to the throne of Spain, Carlos VII. Bradomín is really the only memorable character in the novel; neither his friends nor his enemies, nor even the women who still fall under his spell, are especially memorable. He is truly alone now, a weak and sad old man whose arrogance has come to border on the ridiculous. The whiteness of his hair mimics the snow on the ground and the coldness of the air foreshadows his approaching death. His valor undiminished, Bradomín campaigns on behalf of a cause that venerates history, tradition, and sovereignty by divine right. And, though such dedication to lost causes results in the amputation of his left arm, Bradomín is consoled by royalty, old loves, and even his own illegitimate daughter whom he tries to seduce and drive to take her own life. On the whole, however, love is supplanted as the main theme by gallantry, with religion and patriotism as the most important subthemes. The omnipresence of a pathetic fallacy motif, where the setting seems to be a psychic projection of the character's inner self, dominates the entirety of the *Winter Sonata*. The gray light, the cold, the monotony of sunless and snowy days, and the privations of the royalist troops all point to an end that cannot be far away for either the Marqués de Bradomín or the pretender Carlos VII's struggle for the crown.

The *Sonatas,* perfect miniatures that they are, have aged nonetheless and in a sense become *demodé* as a result of the changes in readers' sensibilities. They are admirable, though perhaps more so as museum pieces than anything else. It fell to Valle himself to begin deriding the *Sonatas.* He called them "light violin music, and bad music even at that"[17] years later, making it easy for others to comment in a similar vein. But, in fact, they represent Spanish modernist prose at its best and constitute Valle's earliest masterpieces. The *Sonatas* are lovingly crafted novelettes whose perfection approaches that of a poem: musical from the title to the last paragraph, they are colorful in accord with the season and the protagonists' consciousness (mauve and green predominate in *Autumn;* white and grey in *Winter;* blue and red in *Spring;* red and yellow in *Summer*); lyrical in their vocabulary and syntax, they are exquisite in the choice of emotions exhibited, and sentimental in the memories of love and bygone times. Their subjectivity is sympathetic to the hero's way of life and, finally, their symbolism is myriad in its range from the oneiric to the satanic.

The Carlist War

The novels of the Carlist War cycle represent an uneasy interlude in Valle's fiction. The public did not like them, the critics have paid little attention to them, and Valle would later reverse the partisan ideological attitude expressed in *Los cruzados de la causa* (The crusaders for the cause), *El resplandor de la hoguera* (The bonfire's glow), and *Gerifaltes de antaño* (Gerfalcons of yore), the first one dating from 1908 and the last two from 1909. Perhaps they do not measure up to the artistic level of the novels that precede or follow them, yet they remain significant in Valle's production for several reasons. First of all, they are inhabited in part and to a great extent by familiar characters encountered in earlier works—Bradomín, Isabel, Cara de Plata, Don Juan Manuel Montenegro, Roquito the sexton, and others—who will appear in future ones. This in itself is of some interest since their character development can be studied as they act in different settings and circumstances. Second, these Carlist War novels are the first stage in a transition of aesthetics from the idealized perspective of the *Sonatas* to the grotesquerie of the later *esperpentos:* a progression of aesthetics from idealism *(Sonatas)* through realism (Carlist novels) to absurd expressionism (the *esperpento* novels). And finally, the Carlist War trilogy figures in the study of Valle's fiction because it demonstrates its author's interest in novelistic format and his willingness to experiment. Whereas the *Sonatas* centered around the figure of a single protagonist, the Marqués de Bradomín, the novels of the Carlist War lack a central figure or even a dominant one—except for the third novel—and instead advance the notion of a multiple protagonist. Together with a collectivism of characters, Valle introduces an episodic fragmentation that precludes linear narrative development. There are juxtaposed and parallel scenes as well as a few sequential ones, but extended periods of continuity rarely exist in any of these novels.

The three novels were written in the span of two years. The first one, *Los cruzados de la causa,* begins where the last *Sonata,* the *Winter Sonata,* left off, during the campaigns of Carlos VII in the last Carlist War, which spanned the years 1872 to 1876. Valle considered these works as belonging as much to the realm of history as to the realm of fiction. In them he sought to idealize and immortalize the Carlist ideology in which he is thought to have believed fervently at the time. Valle shared this partisan attitude in *Los cruzados de la causa* with Bardomín who, because of his sacrifices for Carlism, becomes a more human and likeable character. This is the only one of the three novels that takes place in Galicia and in the Marqués's estate of Viana del Prior, a familiar setting affording the author a head start in the presentation of characters and in the fostering of a warlike atmosphere.

Perhaps dissatisfied with a lack of firsthand knowledge of the embattled territories, Valle journeyed to Navarra before finishing the last two works of the series. There he interviewed veterans of the campaign, among them the leaders Marichalar, Elío, and Valdespina,[18] and walked about some of the battlefields. Not unexpectedly, *El resplandor de la hoguera* and *Gerifaltes de antaño* are set in these Basque latitudes. In them, Valle's novelistic concept of the war continues to unfold as the actions multiply in diverse scenarios. The impression is that of a popular epic where mostly villagers and rural people take up the fight. Even in the most singly protagonized work, *Gerifaltes de antaño* (a title derived from Rubén Darío's poem "Los cisnes" [The swans]), the guerilla leader Manuel Santa Cruz, a former priest, is viewed primarily as a man of the country, a farmer. This reflects Valle's illusory hope of preserving old traditions by means of a popular uprising, though at the same time it points to a social blindness whereby the nobility and the landed gentry would keep all of their privileges and wealth, while the poor and the farmers would gain none. The aesthetic solution as Valle presents it is that the poor fight for religious reasons ("I'd rather have him dead than crucifying our Lord Jesus Christ,"[19] says a woman whose son is shot while fleeing the Republican army that drafted him; the implication being that Republicans are soulless men while Carlists are God-fearing Christians) and the powerful fight for their titles and their lands. The old aristocracy will go on protecting its serfs. In none of it is there any discernible irony. Valle in the novels of the Carlist War believes in the sanctity of the status quo.

All of the episodes into which the three novels are fragmented pit the aristocracy and the poor against the Republicans. The latter are a homogeneous band characterized by the greatness of their numbers, the sufficiency of their armaments and provisions, and the hatred they inspire. The Carlists, though viewed much more heterogeneously, are fewer in number but brave, respectful of God, women, and country (i.e., tradition), and supported by the populace. One scene in *Los cruzados de la causa* succeeds in depicting all of the Republicans' cardinal sins when their soldiers march into a convent in search of a hidden cache of arms. In so doing they have desecrated a church (antireligious), violated the nuns' safety (anti-women), and showed disrespect toward the abbess (antiaristocracy since she happens to be Isabel *{Autumn Sonata}*, the noble cousin of Bradomín). The aesthetics of the novels of the Carlist War may have been compromised by Valle's often seemingly contrived partisan Carlist sympathies, which in part helps to explain the relative low esteem in which they have always been held. On the other hand, it is interesting to note that the new aesthetic toward which he was moving at this time, the *esperpento*, is no less emphatic in its advancement of a sociopolitical ideology quite opposed to that of the

Carlist novels; the major difference lies in the greater human, realistic, and universal scope of Valle's evolving ideology.

Tierra Caliente: A Banana Republic

Busy with his dramas and theater productions, Valle had not published a novel for seventeen years when in 1926 *Tirano Banderas: Novela de Tierra Caliente (The Tyrant: A Novel of the Tropics)* appeared in bookstores. At the age of sixty, Valle had written his greatest novel; thereafter this genre was to be his sole occupation and interest. Widely acclaimed from the very beginning, *The Tyrant* is firmly entrenched in the *esperpento* aesthetic in which Valle found room to criticize as well as to create—a reformist mode of literary expression based on what Julián Marías calls "intrinsic commentary,"[20] by which he means that Valle's narrative fashion carries with it, implicitly, a commentary or a judgment that interprets or colors the reality at hand.

Between 1909, the publication date of his last novel *Gerifaltes de antaño,* and 1926, the year of *The Tyrant,* Valle had returned to Mexico, invited by President Alvaro Obregón who put at Valle's disposal a railroad car in which the writer was free to crisscross the country. It was during this long and pleasant visit that Valle's earlier plans (on the 1909 cover jacket of *El resplandor de la hoguera* he had claimed to have in press [!] another novel titled *Hernán Cortés*)[21] began to take a more definitive turn. As in the case of the earlier Carlist novels, he may have felt the need to further document himself before attempting its actual writing. Written about one year after his return from Mexico, Valle's letters to his friend the Mexican author Alfonso Reyes (1889–1959)—then in Madrid as his country's cultural attaché—show a continued desire to investigate further other aspects of Mexican history, especially concerning the lives of Francisco Madero and Teresa Utrera, whom he had in mind as possible characters.[22] In a 14 November, 1923 letter to Reyes, the title of the novel is finally set as *Tirano Banderas.*[23] From this brief amount of data, it can be concluded that Valle was at work on *The Tyrant* for several years. It had to be a slow process of elaboration, so complex are its structure, its language, and its symbolism—difficulties that have forestalled popular recognition of its worth in spite of the critical acclaim accorded to it.

The Tyrant tells the story of the crazed dictator Santos Banderas (also known as Tirano Banderas and El tigre de Zamalpoa) who rules the apocryphal Latin American nation of Tierra Caliente (literally "hot land") with ruthless disregard for human dignity. Set in the year 1873, the events in the novel take place during three days— a briefness of time belied by the extensiveness of the work. Structurally, *The Tyrant* is devised according to a cabalistic arrangement that corresponds to the internal meaning of the work. Based on the numbers three and seven, the novel is divided into seven parts of which the first three and the last three are further subdivided into three books, whereas the middle section or part 4 has seven books.[24] The folkloric, superstitious, and magical properties attached to these numbers is well-known, and Valle further makes use of them not only in the already mentioned three-day period of the action, but also in the seven parts in which the tyrant appears throughout the novel, in the three parts in which each of the several main characters (Roque Cepeda, the Spanish minister, Quintín Pereda, and Sánchez Ocaña) also appear, in the three social classes treated (Creole, Indian, black), and in countless occurrences involving the numbers three and seven. Such numerical rhythm sets the stage for the viewing of an atavistic society, not at all where it should be in terms of a civilized political climate. The overall structure of the novel, likewise tripartite, offers a sample of the chronological disorder operating throughout *The Tyrant*. The prologue's events happen after those narrated in the novel itself and come before the climax, which occurs in the epilogue—a circular symbolism also manifested when the tyrant's friends gather around him always in a circle, or when the Harris Circus is the scene for political caucusing. More often than not, however, the composition of *The Tyrant* suggests a cubist painting where episodes sometimes are synchronous, at others intrude into one another, and at still others are cut, suddenly interrupted, only to resume at a later time.

Just as Tierra Caliente represents a collage of many Latin American republics, Santos Banderas is a composite of the archetypal cruel tyrant. In the cited correspondence[25] to Alfonso Reyes, Valle suggests that Argentina's Juan Manuel Rosas, Paraguay's Dr. Francia, and Mexico's Porfirio Díaz served as models for Santos Banderas, but other countries and their leaders could have served equally well: Ecuador's Gabriel García Moreno and Guatemala's Estrada Cabrera among them. Because Valle was more familiar with Mexico, one tends to think of Porfirio Díaz as the likeliest of the lot, especially in view of the fact that the name of the Indian Zacarías San José's dog—whose plate he shares—is also Porfirio. In any event, Valle regrettably did not lack for models to inspire him. The name Santos Banderas (loosely translated as "holy flags"), parodically and by antonomasia alludes to the dual source of his power, the Catholic church and the army, which traditionally have been the bastions of government support for centuries in Latin America. In consonance, the tyrant's regime is ultrarightist, and Santos himself is an ascetic, almost puritanical individual who chooses as his headquarters the monastery of San Martín de los Mostenses—ironically, the patron saint of the poor in Catholic hagiography.

This semisuperstitious climate is heightened by the religious festivities of All Souls and All Saints days, celebrated in the course of the novel. In the thick of these November holy days, the political situation grows more untenable by the hour. As the novel opens, Santos Banderas, ruler of Tierra Caliente for the past fifteen years, is returning from the city of Zamalpoa where he has just quashed an uprising. Unbeknownst to the tyrant, however, another attempt to overthrow him, led by the Creole Filomeno Cuevas, is about to take place. In the midst of this chaos Valle plies his craft as a satirical analyst of a whole society, which he has divided again into three segments: the Indians, the Creoles, and the Gachupines. And, though Santos Banderas forms part of the first group, it is the last group—the Spaniards—who come off least well: the Spanish minister is a drug addict and a homosexual, the wealthiest Spaniard is an odious moneylender, the minister's lover is a down-and-out matador, and many others are caricatured sycophants of the tyrant, supporting him for fear that a change in rule would mean an end to their illicit profits reaped from the slavery of the Indians and their extensive control of mineral riches.

In the end the revolution succeeds in unseating the tyrant. Santos Banderas, aware of what awaits him, slits the throat of his own daughter—far more insane than he but infinitely less malignant—to keep her from his enemies' hands, and, after he himself is shot to death, his body is quartered and publicly displayed in the country's largest cities. Death to him who not only had degraded and enslaved but also tortured and killed so many others is Valle's final sentence, and one that encapsulates the novel's main themes of suffering and death.

The Tyrant, though difficult reading because of its fragmented and disparate structure and its colloquial language—slang from Bolivia, Chile, Mexico, and the Plate River countries[26]—is immensely rich in its depiction and satire of an entire society that owed many of both its virtues and its sins to Spain. It is to Valle's credit to lay the blame squarely on those upon whom it belonged. Years later the Latin American authors themselves, prominent among them Miguel Angel Asturias (1899–1974) with *El Señor Presidente* (Mr. President, 1946), would use *The Tyrant* as a model for their own novels dealing with the same themes of power, corruption, and death.

The Catholic Church, the Monarchy, and the Bullring

The series *El ruedo ibérico* (The Iberian ring) was to have been Valle's longest and most ambitious novelistic project. In fact, it was his last. Of the planned three series of three (that number again) novels each, only two of the first group were completed before Valle's death. A third incomplete one was published posthumously in book form in 1958. Valle conceived the cycle in the form of three trilogies: the first one titled *Los amenes de un reinado* (The last gasps of a reign) was to include *La corte de los milagros* (The court of miracles), *Viva mi dueño* (Hurrah for my owner), and *Baza de espadas* (Round of spades); the second series was titled "Aleluyas de la gloriosa" (Hallelujah for the revolution) and its volumes were to be "España con honra" (Spain with honor), "Trono en ferias" (The throne in fairs), and "Fueros y cantones" (Rights and counties); the third series, "La restauración borbónica" (The Bourbon return) was to contain these three books: "Los salones alfonsinos" (King Alfonso's salons), "Dios, Patria, Rey" (God, country, king), and "Los campos de Cuba" (The Cuban fields).

Though the completed two novels and the unfinished (though published) remnants of the third are linked in subject matter and characters—Bradomín reappears—to the novels of the Carlist War, *El ruedo ibérico* is much closer in technique and ideological content to *The Tyrant*. The name of the series clearly alludes to the circular structure managed in threes previously seen in the novel of "Tierra Caliente", but it also evokes the whole of Spain in terms of a bullring with all of the attendant factors attached to Spaniards' favorite form of entertainment—a circus atmosphere. With the country thus initially debased, Valle spins in these volumes a moral and critical history that, regardless of being set in the nineteenth century, has much to do with the time in which he was writing. The only extant trilogy takes place in the last year of Queen Isabel II's reign, previously not merely a secondary figure in the Carlist novels but also a principal character in the 1922 play *Farsa y licencia de la Reina Castiza* (Farce of the Castilian queen). *Los amenes de un reinado* begins on the eve of the 1868 Revolution, called "la Niña" (The Little Girl) by everyone, from the fourth Sunday in Lent until a few days after 9 August—approximately six months.[27] This revolution is triggered by the queen's heeding the counsel of her ill-intentioned religious advisers—Sister Patrocinio (a stigmata popularly known as "The Bleeding Nun"), Padre Claret (note the oenanthic irony), and others of their ilk—plus the reaction of the slighted army generals who acted in their own best interests rather than in their country's.[28]

"La corte de los milagros" (The court of miracles), as Isabel's government was called because of the undue religious influence on the throne, also echoed the medieval Parisian host of prostitutes, beggars, and assassins known by the same title. "Viva mi dueño" (Hurrah for my owner), the motto inscribed on the switchblade knives commonly wielded by criminals, is here transposed onto generals' swords. *Baza de espadas* (Round of spades) is a title that by dint of a synecdoche turns generals into swords, these into spades, and all of their doings into a mere card game. These interpretative titles chronicle the instability and rapid decline of the queen's tenure throughout Spain, but mainly in and around the capital city of Madrid. As in the earlier 1908–9 Carlist War novels, there is no single protagonist in *El ruedo ibérico,* though some characters such as Isabel II, her lover Adolfito Bonifaz, and the Marqués de Torre Mellada stand out above the rest. The true protagonist, once again, is the era and its people, seen in brief, almost disconnected, chapters that painfully detail the depth of the corruption and lawlessness in the upper reaches of Spanish society—from the cretinous Isabel II to her murderous minions. In a bleak panorama Valle introduces character after character who is weak, frivolous, hypocritical, and immoral: *guardias civiles* (rural police) who shoot a train passenger for riding without a ticket or kill a cripple trying to escape, aristocratic youths who throw a policeman to his death from an upper-story balcony on a dare, and a queen who hopes to save her soul by appeasing her confessor. In these instances and more Valle's vitriolic prose points an accusing finger at Spain's two worst enemies within: the Catholic church and the government—an unholy alliance seeking to perpetuate its power and extend its dominance at the expense of the country's future and that of its people.

Valle did not enjoy the popularity that Baroja's large readership conferred upon the latter. During Valle's lifetime his poetry was almost unknown and many of his dramas were not staged until long after he had died. Unlike some of his contemporaries who gained either critical or public approval and at times both, Valle did not have a loyal constituency from either group until very late. In part this anomaly may be attributed to the evolving nature of his art, which precluded an easy critical appraisal on the one hand and a comfortable mass following on the other. Neither critics nor reading public could ever feel comfortable with Valle's books. He changed continuously and shocked often. The trajectory of his production, initially described as a progression from mere aestheticism to a fiction where aesthetics functions as a genuinely felt set of ethics, may have prevented Valle from gaining an immediate and large audience. In the end it matters little. Since his death Valle has risen above most of his contemporaries, not only in the esteem of his novelistic production but also in his stature as a poet and a dramatist of the highest order.

Chapter Five

Ramón Pérez de Ayala: The Intellectual Novel

Ramón Pérez de Ayala eminently personifies a new generation of writers, more elitist than those of the preceeding Generation of 1898, discussed in chapters 2–4, and more self-assured in their international standing, though no less inclined to look inward to Spain for the main concerns of their works. These men were all university educated; some had other professional concerns (such as medicine, teaching, and publishing) besides writing, and most made Madrid their home—and thus Spain's cultural center—from the turn of the century until the outbreak of the Civil War in 1936.

The Generation of 1914

The acrostic MAJO (in Andalusian argot, "good looking"), aside from incorporating the initials of the members of this new generation, is also a tell-tale sign of their success both as writers and as well-to-do, influential personalities who guided Spain's intellectual fortunes for over a quarter century. They were the novelist Gabriel Miró (1879–1930), the physician and essayist Gregorio Marañón (1887–1960), Ayala himself (1880–1962), the educator and novelist Benjamín Jarnés (1888–1950), the Nobel Prize–winning poet Juan Ramón Jiménez (1881–1958), and the philosopher and publisher José Ortega y Gasset (1883–1955). They constitute on the whole a more intellectual group than the Generation of 1898, especially when one considers the breadth of an upbringing that for most of them included studies abroad in Germany, Italy, France, and England together with travels throughout the European continent and the Americas as well. Their educations were at the hands of the most demanding and rigorous teachers of the times—the Jesuits—against whom they later rebelled, but to whom they owed their profound knowledge of Greek, Latin, the classics, philosophy, and theology. Most of them came from upper-middle-class families who could afford these colleges, the trips beyond Spain's borders, and finance careers that would lead to lucrative medical practices, ambassadorships, and publishing empires.

The MAJO writers were a generation of thinkers who did not approach the world of letters with a deliberate intent to change the course of events in the same way that their literary ancestors had done initially, but instead chose to manifest themselves in more cerebral, less entertaining writings: Unamuno's egocentrism is thrown over for Ayala's universal mythological parodies; Baroja's sentimental accounts are denounced by Ortega's new concept of the novel, which he called "dehumanization";[1] Valle's sociopolitical diatribes are softened by Miró's aesthetic distances. Their extraliterary preoccupations and occupations explain the paucity of their output, especially in comparison with Baroja's sixty-odd novels and the scores of other writings that bring the number of his complete works to nearly one hundred volumes. The three novelists of the Generation of 1914 combined did not write as much as he. Ayala, Miró, and Jarnés each wrote fewer than a dozen major novels, and the total of their minor novels is of a similar magnitude. None of these novelists are much concerned with telling a story in the way Baroja, Valle, or even Unamuno may have been. Theirs is a novel of ideas—full of digressions, at times lyrical, at others essayistic—which, though challenging to the well-educated individual, tends to drive the majority of readers to distraction and even despair. Thus Ayala, Miró, and Jarnés were slowly abandoned by the masses and became novelists of a minority that was willing to ponder these fictional challenges to its intelligence.

The Life of Ramón Pérez de Ayala

So little is known of Ayala's early years that even his birthdate is open to debate among critics.[2] The likeliest consensus fixes it in the first part of August of 1880, although Ayala himself would have us believe it to be 1881. No doubt, however, exists concerning the place of birth—it was Oviedo, the same Asturian capital that his teacher Leopoldo Alas, "Clarín" (1852–1901), fictionalized as Vetusta in *La Regenta* (1884), and that Ayala himself would call Pilares in most of his fiction. Born into a wealthy family, the young Ramón began his education at age eight with the Jesuits, initially in Carrión de los Condes (Palencia) and two years later in their college at the city of Gijón until 1894. These six years left an indelible emotional stain on the spirit of Pérez de Ayala. Embittered and resentful of the cruel and capricious pedagogical methods employed by the Order, Ayala would later fictionalize this experience into a thinly disguised attack against the Jesuits in his second novel, *A.M.D.G.* At the San Zoilo school (Carrión de los Condes) he was fortunate, however, to have as one of his teachers the compassionate Julio Cejador y Frauca (1864–1927), who would eventually leave the Jesuits to become an eminent philologist and literary historian. After six years of study at the University of Oviedo, Ayala emerged as an attorney in 1901. Not particularly distinguished as a student, he would remember with special fondness his professor of canon law, Leopoldo Alas, already famous for his masterpiece novel *La Regenta* and for his influential book reviews in Madrid's major newspapers. Clarín, a figure he admired greatly, would eventually respect his disciple's own merits, and with reason, for in later years Ayala was to be known as his literary successor.

In the summer of 1901, Ayala left his hometown of Oviedo to enroll in the University of Madrid's Ph.D. program at the College of Law. He was by this time a man of curious intellect with a formidable education in the classics and in law. He also could count on his father's financial backing either to further his education or to begin his law practice. As the months passed, however, Ayala found himself more often than not in the company of writers and other intellectuals more interested in the vagaries of endless political and literary pursuits than in the more practical side of life. He began to publish short articles in small, now-defunct journals, some of which he helped found, such as *Helios* (with Juan Ramón Jiménez), *Renacimiento, Alma Española,* and *Europa.* Ayala's earliest coup came on 1 February, 1904 when his first short story, "Quería morir" (Wanting to die), was carried by no less a newspaper than *El Imparcial,* Madrid's most prestigious daily. In that same year Ayala also published his first book of poetry, one of four, titled *La paz del sendero* (The peaceful path), whose modernist verses were highly praised by his friend, the Nicaraguan poet Rubén Darío.

His career as a writer—not as an attorney—now launched, Ayala followed these early successes with the novel *Tinieblas en las cumbres* (Darkness on the heights) in 1907 and with travels abroad as a foreign correspondent for *El Imparcial.* This carefree, almost bohemian, existence changed suddenly, however, when in February 1908

Ayala's father, Cirilo, committed suicide rather than face bank-ruptcy. Returning from London, Ayala realized that for the first time ever he had to face life's economic realities without his family's fortune. Instead he could now rely only on his solid education and the power of his capable intellect. Both served him well as he almost immediately secured a grant to study art in Florence, following the publication of *A.M.D.G.* in 1911. In this Italian Renaissance center he met the American Mabel Rick, a music student. They parted ways, she to the United States, he to Germany with another fel-lowship, in the fall of 1912. That year *La pata de la raposa (The Fox's Paw)* was published, and while in Germany Ayala managed to finish his fourth novel, *Troteras y danzaderas* (Mummers and dancers). In late summer of 1913 Ayala journeyed to America where on 1 September he married Mabel Rick in Allentown, Pennsylvania. The couple remained in the United States several months, during which Ayala continued sending articles to *El Imparcial* (later collected in part in the book *El país del futuro: Mis viajes a los Estados Unidos, 1913–1914; 1919–1920* [The country of the future: my journeys to the United States, 1913–1914; 1919–1920]), before returning to live in Spain. A sympathizer of the Allies at the outbreak of World War I, Ayala reported on the conflict for the Buenos Aires daily *La Prensa*. His numerous journalistic collaborations plus the income derived from the sales of his books enabled the Ayalas to enjoy a comfortable economic situation. With their children Juan and Eduardo, they lived on number 11 Espalter Street near the Madrid Botanical Gardens and the beautiful Retiro Park. Their yearly vacations were spent in the village of Riaza (Segovia) above Madrid and away from its stifling summer heat.

The end of World War I in 1918 brought with it time for Ayala to spend on longer works; with the three short poematic novels, *Prometeo (Prometheus), Luz de domingo (Sunday Sunlight),* and *La caída de los Limones (The Fall of the House of Limón),* a second book of poetry *El sendero innumerable* (The path of infinite variations), plus four books of essays, *Hermann encadenado* (Hermann bound), *Las máscaras* (The masks), and *Política y toros* (Politics and bulls), behind him, Ayala embarked on the writing of his major novels. In the five years 1921 to 1926 Ayala managed to publish, aside from a third volume of poetry, *El sendero andante* (The flowing path), and two more collections of short stories, *El ombligo del mundo* (The navel of the world) and *Bajo el signo de Artemisa* (Under the sign of Artemisa), all of his major novels. These are three full-length works, two of which are bipartite novels: *Belarmino y Apolonio; Luna de miel, Luna de hiel (Honeymoon, Bittermoon)* and its sequel *Los trabajos de Urbano y Simona (The Trials of Urbano y Simona);* and *Tigre Juan (Tiger Juan)* and its sequel *El curandero de su honra* (The healer of his honor). This last one earned him Spain's first National Prize for Literature in 1926, the year of its publication.

In 1928 Ayala was elected to the Spanish Royal Academy, his nation's highest literary honor, but he never read his inaugural speech, remaining a member-elect. After the issuing of a minor short novel, *Justicia* (Justice), in this same year, he never published another book of fiction. Ayala turned again to journalism and increasingly to politics. He was elected to the Parliament of Spain's Second Republic upon the forced abdication of King Alfonso XIII. A liberal antimonarchist, Ayala joined Ortega and Marañón to form the "Agrupación de Intelectuales al Servicio de la República" (League for the Defense of the Republic). For a brief period he served as the director of the Prado Museum, an appointment that, while no doubt politically motivated, took into account Ayala's fondness for art and his earlier desire to become a painter (several of his watercolors survive to this day). Then on 22 May, 1931 he was named Spain's ambassador to Great Britain, a post he held until 1936, when he resigned at the outbreak of the Civil War. In the three-year period (1936–39) that the conflict lasted, Ayala lived in exile in France (Paris and Biarritz), and in early 1940 he established residency in Buenos Aires. There he remained for nearly fifteen years, writing essays and lecturing to supplement his retirement salary from the Franco government through its Argentine embassy as befitting a former ambassador.[3]

On 20 December, 1954 the Ayala family returned to Spain. In Madrid Ayala became a forgotten literary figure, breaking his silence only to appear sporadically in print in the essay pages of the arch-conservative daily *ABC*. In 1957 an expurgated version of his *Obras selectas* (Selected works) appeared in Barcelona without much fanfare. Ayala's last significant moment on the Spanish literary scene came in 1960 when he was awarded the prestigious and economically generous Juan March Prize for Creative Writing. He died almost a recluse on 5 August, 1962 at the age of eighty-two.

Ayala's Aesthetics and Novelistic Classification

In Ayala's aesthetics an art-literature duality constantly coexists. As previously mentioned, he was fond of paintings; in his Madrid apartment Ayala collected fine canvases—not only those of his contemporaries (some of whom did his portrait) like Sorolla (1863–1923), Zuloaga (1870–1945), and Vázquez Díaz (1882–1962) among them—but also such classics as Murillo (1618–82). It should be remembered also that he studied art in Florence, the world's major center of Renaissance culture, that he was the director of the Prado Museum in the early 1930s, that he painted while in exile in Argentina, and that he wrote numerous essays on the subject of art.

The first two lines of Antonio Machado's iconographic sonnet "Ramón Pérez de Ayala," which appears in *Nuevas canciones* (New songs, 1924)—"Lo recuerdo. . . . Un pintor me lo retrata, / no en el lino, en el tiempo . . . " I remember him. . . . A painter does his portrait, / Not on canvas, [but] in time . . . —allude to his writer-painter duality. The writer's is a time art; the painter's, a space art. Ayala felt that prior fiction had portrayed or interpreted life in a two-dimensional fashion. Dissatisfied, he wanted to add another dimension to fiction that would infuse it with more lifelike qualities. His is an experimental literature that strives to provide that extra dimension evoking more verisimilitude via numerous devices: the landscapes in *Tinieblas en las cumbres* and *The Fox's Paw,* his romans á clef; nature in *Troteras y danzaderas;* the symbolic and complementary poems accompanying *Prometheus, Sunday Sunlight,* and *The Fall of the House of Limón;* the juxtaposed and simultaneous scenes of *Belarmino y Apolonio,* as well as this novel's multiple points of view; and the classical and mythological replay or mirroring in almost all of his works that seek not to complicate or confuse the reading but, instead, to add depth of time, distance, and meaning.

That Ayala published no fiction after 1928 may be due in part to the fact that he was busy with politics, journalism, and the trials of exile, or that he was merely lazy (his usual waking hour was noon);[4] but I believe it also had to do with his inability to make further progress in the art of the novel. Ayala may have felt that with *Belarmino y Apolonio,* his antepenultimate work, he had reached his own unsurpassable outer limit. And it is true that neither *The Novels of Urbano and Simona* nor the bipartite *Tiger Juan* and *El curandero de su honra* progress beyond *Belarmino y Apolonio* in any novelistic dimension. Ayala knew he could not transcend his last novel, written at age forty-five, and for the last thirty-six years of his life he remained silent on the subject.

Ayala belongs to the Spanish novelistic lineage of Juan Valera (1824–1905), Leopoldo Alas (Clarín), his university professor, and Miguel de Unamuno, his friend.[5] Like them he was a liberal and a skeptic; his fiction, much like theirs, was experimental and showed a tragicomic aspect of life, and like them he was steeped in the classics as well as in his own country's literature. The anticlerical, though not antireligious, attitude of the four is similar, as seen in certain works such as Valera's *Pepita Jiménez* (1874), Clarín's *La Regenta*, Unamuno's *Saint Manuel Bueno, Martyr*, and especially Ayala's own *A.M.D.G.* And yet, strictly speaking, Ayala cannot be said to belong to any school. He served no direct apprenticeship with any of the above authors, and though their ideas may have had much in common, the nature of their writing (structure, theme, characterization, style) was different. Nor did Ayala leave behind any disciples. He was a loner both as a writer and as a man.

Ayala wrote three collections of short stories, *La araña* (The spider, 1913), *Bajo el signo de Artemisa* (Under Artemisa's sign, 1924), and *El Raposín* (The small fox, 1962), aside from his ten minor short novels and seven major novels—the last group produced over a period of approximately two decades (1907–28). He wrote quickly and with confidence, judging by his statement, "Todas las novelas las he escrito en un mes cada una" ("I've written all of my novels in one month"),[6] and by the lack of corrections observable in the manuscripts he left behind.[7]

The novels of Ramón Pérez de Ayala are best classified into three groupings that initially appear to heed only a chronological order, but that subsequently reveal intrinsic reasons for such a tripartite classification. The first period of Ayala's novelistic career is made up of four full-length works: *Tinieblas en las cumbres, A.M.D.G., The Fox's Paw*, and *Troteras y danzaderas*. These are mainly autobiographical works, centering on the author's alter ego, Alberto Díaz de Guzmán, as he grows and attempts to resolve the spiritual crises of his youth. The middle period in the development of Ayala's novel corresponds to the years in which he wrote *Prometheus, Sunday Sunlight*, and *The Fall of the House of Limón*. Jointly published in one volume under the subtitle *Poematic Novels about Spanish Life,* these are considered transitional pieces, lyrical in style and pessimistic in tone.

From 1916, date of publication of the poematic novels, until 1921 Ayala published no new novels. In these intervening five years Ayala wrote and published his three most important collections of essays: *Hermann encadenado,* on World War I; *Las Máscaras,* two volumes on drama; and *Política y toros.* Ayala wrote five major novels—beginning in 1921 and in the five years that followed—four of which must be considered as two bipartite works. These are all mature works, intellectual and philosophical masterpieces that critics have ranked on a par with Cervantes's *Don Quixote,*[8] Flaubert's *Bevard et Pecuchet,*[9] and Joyce's *Ulysses.*[10] To this group belong *Belarmino y Apolonio, Honeymoon, Bitter Moon,* and its sequel, *The Trials of Urbano and Simona,* as well as *Tiger Juan* and its second part, *El curandero de su honra.*

The Autobiographical Novels

The four novels belonging to the first period of Ayala's production are largely documentary and biographical, and to an even greater degree autobiographical. All are episodic since the narrative thread is constantly fragmented into a series of nearly autonomous scenes, vignettes that can best be described as anthology pieces—perfectly understandable almost unto themselves. The characters that appear in one reappear in the others with varying role importance. They, along with Alberto Díaz de Guzmán, the protagonist of the tetralogy, lend the four books an air of continuity. In fact, the autobiographical novels can fittingly be labeled an extended bildungsroman in which the maturation of the hero is chronicled from his adolescent school days to his economic emancipation in the big city.

The first of these novels, *Tinieblas en las cumbres,* was written in 1905 though not published until 1907. It is followed by *A.M.D.G.,* a title alluding to the Jesuit Order's motto "Ad Maiorem Dei Gloriam" (To the Greater Glory of God), in 1910. *The Fox's Paw* and *Troteras y danzaderas* came in 1912 and 1913, respectively. However, this chronological order of publication does not correspond to the internal chronology of the works that unfolds in the sequence: *A.M.D.G., Tinieblas en las cumbres, Troteras y danzaderas,* and *The Fox's Paw.*

Though Ayala's first novel, *Tinieblas en las cumbres,* was well received by critics and public alike, *A.M.D.G.,* his second, made him famous. The reasons for such notoriety, however, were not strictly literary. *A.M.D.G.* created a publishing scandal. It was both applauded and deplored with equal determination by those who took it as literature, as well as by those others who saw it as a document. The theme, religious education in Spain and particularly that of the Jesuit Order, and its treatment caused the furor. The novel recounts the misfortunes that befall the young orphan Bertuco (Alberto), whose mother has died and whose father has abandoned him to an uncle, as he is left at the Jesuit College of the Immaculate Conception in Regium by his old nanny for the duration of the school year. The author presents a detailed account of the Jesuits and their pedagogical, religious, and economic practices (e.g., how to influence the wealthy and the infirm to ensure that their last wills and testaments will be on the Order's behalf), practices that in almost every case seem contrary to Christian precepts. For them the end always justifies the means; their rewards inevitably foster betrayal, secretiveness, and deceit. The priests depicted are cruel, vengeful, and given to sophistry. The most tyrannical are dehumanized by the animal appellations: Father Mur (mouse), Father Conejo (rabbit). The very few priests who are favorites of the children and are liked by the townspeople are ostracized by the rest of the Order. Among them is Father Atienza, a wise, kind, and humorous man, who never leaves his cell—not even to teach class.

Although Bertuco discovers his gifts as an artist and because of his intellectual prowess is awarded a medal by his teachers, the intimidating and closed atmosphere of the monastery school weighs heavily on him. He becomes increasingly introspective and in a diary entry reveals how perverted his spiritual beliefs have become. In this fourteenth and penultimate chapter, Bertuco expresses his belief that God punishes without forgiving, wishing not to be loved but to be feared. Motherless and conscious of his father's estrangement from him, Bertuco directs all of his fervor and devotion to the Virgin, whom he sees not only as kind but also forgiving.

The novel concludes prior to the end of the school year, precipitated by Bertuco's leaving the college after becoming ill from a severe beating at the hands of Father Mur (for his reluctance to draw a cross on the floor of the chapel with his tongue). The child is taken away by his uncle Don Alberto and the family doctor, accompanied by Father Atienza who leaves the Order following the Jesuits' refusal to allow publication of his treatise on evolution. That this priests' true identity was that of Julio Cejador, the critic who also left the Jesuit Order, is only one of many clues pointing to the autobiographical nature of *A.M.D.G.* Others are the cross of *emperador* awarded to Ayala which Bertuco receives, Ayala's attendance at the Jesuit College of the Immaculate Conception in Gijón (the Regium of the novel) from 1890 to 1894, and Ayala's declaration of his own religious misgivings at the end of his Jesuit schooling days, which parallels Bertuco's confused and doubting spirit before leaving the Order.

Ortega y Gasset, another product of the Jesuit educational system (at their college in Málaga) and like Ayala a recipient of the cross of merit *(emperador),* lauded the novel and saw it as Ayala had intended it: a plea for a more liberal, secular, and enlightened education in Spain. Twenty years after its publication, *A.M.D.G.* was still being argued about. In November 1931 it was staged at the Teatro Beatriz in Madrid; its premiere aroused such violent public reaction that during the first two acts forty-five people were carried off by the police. Among those in the audience were the president of the Spanish Republic, Manuel Azaña, and most of his cabinet; the founder of the Spanish Fascist party, "Falange Española," José Antonio Primo de Rivera; the Soviet ambassador to Spain; and a number of priests. Though it was loudly cheered by those spectators who remained behind, its author could not answer the curtain calls after the last act—he was in London as the Spanish ambassador to Great Britain.

Tinieblas en las cumbres, the second novel of the series and Ayala's first full-length novel, was well enough received by the critics, and the old master Galdós praised it highly in a letter to its author that served as the introduction from its third edition onward. The first edition proclaimed the novel to be the posthumous work of "Plotino Cuevas." Neither its feigned posthumous nature nor the pseudonym fooled many people, though both attest to the scabrous realism of the work, which led several critics of the times to label it a "novela lupanaria" (bawdyhouse novel), charges that Ayala may have anticipated and from which he wished to shield himself.

Tinieblas en las cumbres, less picaresque than Galdós would have it[11] and more erotic than one would have expected for the times, focuses on the unsettled lives of Alberto and Rosina. The novel is

divided into four parts. The inaugural one, "Prolegómenos" (Pre-
liminaries), sets the stage for five young men accompanied by five
prostitutes who are preparing to climb some mountains near Pilares
(Oviedo) in order to observe a solar eclipse. Among them are Alberto
and Rosina. The second part, "El pasado" (The past), tells in flash-
back technique the story of Rosina. This nineteen-year-old prostitute, born into a poor fisherman's family, had rebelled against her
father's wish to marry a rich factory owner and instead had had an
affair and a child with a circus acrobat, obliging her to leave home
and to sell herself for a living.

"La jornada" (The journey), third and longest of the four parts,
relates the trip by train and on foot to the mountain heights. The
abusive drinking, eating, and ribald behavior contrasts with the
lyrical beauty of the mountainous countryside. Affected by the maj-
esty of nature, Alberto does not feel part of the group and avoids
many of the excesses of his companions even though he shows an
interest in Rosina. At the top of the mountain Alberto runs into
Adam Warble (an onomastic significant of untainted paradise), an
English friend to whom he confides that he wants to be an artist
in order to become immortal. Their prolonged dialogue, in which
Yiddy (Warble's nickname) plays the role of a skeptic, leads into
the eclipse whose darkness completely overcomes Alberto. Drunk
and emotionally spent, Alberto conceives this darkness to mean a
snuffing out of his own interior light on which he had counted to
illuminate him through life. Now, thus dejected, he accepts Yiddy's
advice and fully partakes of the group's libidinous and drunken
frolicking. On the way back down the mountain Alberto and Rosina
chance upon a small church whereupon he enters and, still in an
alcoholic incoherence, asks God to return the light of his childhood,
an act that suggests an enduring spiritual crisis. The Epilogue had
appeared in the first edition as the prologue. In it the author Plotino
Cuevas, on his deathbed, turns over to a Jesuit ministering to him
a sheaf of papers (the novel's manuscript) to be published and thus
serve didactically to youths likely to stray from the narrow path.
In the first and subsequent editions this segment is signed by a
Jesuit Father X, ending with the Order's A.M.D.G. anagram. Largely
pessimistic, *Tinieblas en las cumbres* is a drama of conscience and
moral import. Alberto's confused state as an adolescent in search of
a meaning for life or at least a direction to take is not resolved.
Neither is Rosina's unhappy state. Their friends' carefree ways lead

to nothing except the celebration of the present moment in the picaresque fashion, the context in which Galdós suggests the novel should be taken.

The next installments in the lives of Alberto and Rosina appear in *The Fox's Paw* and *Troteras y danzaderas*, two novels inextricably linked in their structural makeup. Part 1, "La noche" ("Night"), of *The Fox's Paw* begins where *Tinieblas en las cumbres* had left off: on the morning after Alberto's return from the raucous drunken excursion to the Pilares mountains. Tormented by remorse and afflicted by a terrible hangover, convinced of the futility of it all, Alberto despairs and proceeds to destroy his paintings and his books. Moreover, accused of Rosina's disappearance in the press and by the police, he flees to his summer cottage of Cenciella where the beauty of the countryside and of his domestic animals once again fills him with solace. In poems to his cat, his rooster, and a humble ant Alberto recognizes and envies their bucolic existence, nearer to paradise than his own. He then seeks a rekindling of the love shared with Fina, his old sweetheart. Encouraged by her aunt Anastasia, they fall in love again, only to have their happiness spoiled when Alberto and his future brother-in-law, on the urging of the latter, visit a bordello one night, an experience that leaves Alberto feeling unworthy of Fina. Turning over his summer house and part of his fortune to his servant, Alberto runs away again. This time he joins a circus, ends up in jail, and is finally exonerated for Rosina's disappearance when she testifies on his behalf.

"El alba"[12] ("Dawn"), the second part of *The Fox's Paw*, finds Alberto in London where he is staying with his friends the MacKenzies to whose daughter, Meg, he feels attracted. While in England he learns that Hurtado (Spanish for "stolen") has absconded with all of his bank funds. This scene, which parallels what in reality had happened to his father causing the elder Ayala's suicide and his son's hurried departure for Spain, forces Alberto's return. Awaiting him is Fina, prepared to marry him but whom he spurns because of his financial exigency. When he arrives at Cenciella Alberto is turned away by his former manservant. Forced to take stock of his situation, Alberto realizes his many mistakes and broods endlessly, unable to act. One day he runs into Fina and her aunt Anastasia who welcome him warmly. Grateful to have their love, Alberto decides to devote himself to Fina, to his work, and to a simpler life. Feeling that he must become worthy of her first, however, Alberto leaves for Madrid to begin anew.

It is at this juncture, between parts two, "Dawn," and three, "La tarde" ("Afternoon"), of *The Fox's Paw*, that the entirety of the novel *Troteras y danzaderas* takes place. Once in Madrid, Alberto quickly forgets about Fina. He begins to write and meets with moderate success, but as he squanders his recovered fortune thoughtlessly, Alberto is forced to share an apartment with Angelón Ríos, a married man whose family lives away in the provinces. Throughout *Torteras y danzaderas* Alberto functions more as an observer and commentator than as the main character.[13] He does fall in love with Verónica, a prostitute who is Angelón's lover, and helps her to become a famous dancer. The protagonist of this novel is the poet and playwright Teófilo Pajares who always complains about life's greatest lacks—according to him, love and money. He is in love with Rosina, the girl from *Tinieblas en las cumbres*, but she is being kept (together with her daughter) by the government minister Sabas Silicia. She leaves him, however, when the circus strongman Fernando, who had fathered her daughter, shows up. In the end Teófilo dies of tuberculosis, Rosina seems happy with Fernando even though he throws away her money at the tables in Paris dance and gambling halls, and Verónica refuses to marry in order to continue her successful career as a dancer in Madrid. Meanwhile, Alberto does not appear any closer to finding himself or his place in the world in *Troteras y danzaderas* than in any of the other novels. Alberto's indecisiveness and lack of courage certainly do not reflect the author's self, but his intellectual curiosity and his sensitivity do give pause when comparing creature and creator.

The title *Troteras y danzaderas* comes from a poem by the four-teenth-century Spanish bard the Archpriest of Hita and summarizes Alberto's estimation of all that Spain has been able to give to the world, nothing but "mummers and dancers." Such is the portrayal of Madrid's bohemian world of the turn of the century, which in Alberto's eyes was largely populated by prostitutes, writers, politicians, and bullfighters, and they may indeed be the true protagonists of this roman á clef. A disparate and desolate urban panorama allows Ayala to mete out enough social criticism to include Spaniards of almost every class and profession, together with such traditional institutions as the church, the state, and the system of education. The many digressions, the multiplicity of themes, and the vast number of characters preclude any possible unity for *Troteras y dan-zaderas*. Instead, a lively and episodic narrative remains, along with an entertaining cast of characters whom Ayala's contemporaries delighted in identifying. Among the twenty-some identifiable ones are Ortega (Antón Tejero), Galdós (Sixto Díaz Torcaz), Valle Inclán (Monte Valdés), Maeztu (Raniero Mazorral), Benavente (Bovadilla), Alvarez Quintero (González Fitoris), and Villaespesa (Teófilo Pajares). Rosina herself is believed to represent the famous dancer "La Fornarina."[14] With equal deftness and accuracy, Ayala described theaters, cafés, and other famous locales of the day.

With the conclusion of *Troteras y danzaderas* and its indictment of Spain's social, political, economic, and intellectual ills, the story line returns to *The Fox's Paw* to continue the theme of the making of an artist. Part 3 of *The Fox's Paw*, "Afternoon," follows the fortunes of Alberto as he seeks to extricate himself from the Madrid scene. After achieving some literary success there and recovering most of his wealth following the imprisonment of the embezzler Hurtado, Alberto moves on to Switzerland. Though unencumbered by the concerns of money, success, and position and now free to marry Fina, he changes his mind and chooses instead to devote his life to every living thing, not just to the "sensual and ephemeral pleasure" signified by one woman. His British friends, the MacKenzies, happen to be in Switzerland also and once more Alberto's attention is drawn to Meg, but in no time he tires of her sexual games and returns to Cenciella. After a three-year absence he is met only by Fina's aunt Anastasia, who announces her niece's death and blames him for it.

The Fox's Paw in its three divisions corresponds to as many turns in the life and spirit of Alberto Díaz Guzmán. The image in its title, alluding to the animal that will sever its leg in order to free itself from a trap, reflects the young man's own trapped state in a past he cannot forget—the period of Jesuit indoctrination—which inflicts constant unhappiness upon him and pain upon others.

The Poematic Novels

In his second novelistic period Ayala discards the autobiographical note, though isolated biographical incidents may still appear, relying instead on a more universal mythology as inspiration for his novels. Accordingly, the works of this period are not as original as the former ones, but their appeal and artistry decidedly make up for any heuristic shortcomings. Subtitled by the author "Novelas poemáticas de la vida española" ("Poematic Novels of Spanish Life"),[15] the trilogy *Prometheus, Sunday Sunlight,* and *The Fall of the House of Limón* was published in 1916 as a single volume. A pessimistic and tragic tone pervades these three novelettes and, though perhaps characteristic of all of Ayala's fiction up to the moment, there is a distinct maturation discernible in this trilogy in the form of a more compact, lyrical, and intellectual narrative.

Prometheus recounts the life of Juan Pérez, a professor of Greek, scholar of Homer, and reincarnation of Odysseus. In this modern re-creation of the Homeric epic poem, Juan Pérez is the son of a handsome but lazy Spanish father and a rich and noble Italian woman. After her death, the widower spends her fortune quickly and then kills himself, an episode recalling Ayala's father's suicide as a result of a large financial loss. Juan is reared by an uncle who had set aside for him a part of his mother's wealth. In a conversation between the two men, the nephew declares that he would like to be not only a man of thought, but also one of action, a dialectic stance that the uncle finds hard to reconcile. Even Juan does not understand how such a goal can be achieved, though he finds himself attracted to both books and booze at the same time. In order to find an answer to his quest Juan goes to Italy, changes his name to Marco, and there samples the pleasures and the treasures of antiquity until satiated when, disenchanted, he returns to Spain. At this juncture, in his mid-thirties, Marco de Setignano (the last name taken from the sculptor Desiderio de Setignano) secures his professorship of Greek language and literature at the University of Pilares (Oviedo, again). Slowly the possibilities he had foreseen begin to disappear and, frustrated, he renounces the ideal duality of action and thought.

The Odyssean dream now begins to give way to the myth of Prometheus. Juan Marco contents himself with pursuits of the mind, settles down to the tranquil life of academia, and searches for the perfect wife to bear him the perfect offspring, a Nietzschean son capable of saving mankind from its follies. In short, Juan Marco wants a Promethean being who will steal the fire (light, intelligence, power) of the gods and bring it to earth. The resemblance to Una- muno's Avito Carrascal and his *Amor y Pedagogía* is inescapable. Both are failed attempts to produce the Nietzschean *(uber-*

mensch)superman—Unamuno's more serious and intellectualized, Ayala's more sarcastic, disillusioned,[16] and literary.

The carnal widow Federica Gómez that he chooses soon turns into the Homeric Calypso from whom Juan Marco (Odysseus) seeks to escape in a homemade raft. Shipwrecked, naked, and hungry, Juan Marco is found on the beach by the maiden Perpetua (Nausikáa), who nurses him back to health. Sensing that Perpetua Meana was destined to become his ideal mate, Juan Marco marries her. The son born to them, though precocious in intelligence, is deformed physically and emotionally. As in Unamuno's *Amor y Pedagogía,* the son Prometheus is discovered one morning hanging from a tree, this time a fig tree. Both novels spoof rational or scientific pedagogical methods. Ayala, however, goes beyond a mere satire since *Prometheus* also reconstructs the enduring literary myths and modernizes them with relevancy. The poems that head each of the five segments—"Rapsodia a manera de prólogo de cómo el moderno Odysseus encontró a la moderna Nausikáa" (Rapsody In the Way of.a Prologue As To How the Modern Odysseus Found the Modern Nausikáa"), "Odysseus," "Nausikáa," "Marco y Perpetua," and "Prometeo"—foreshadow the incidents of each brief chapter in Greek chorus fashion. Though some of the themes in *Prometheus* may be new, such as that of paternity and man's imprisonment in his own age—expressed by the futility of Juan Marco's wishing to be Odysseus—many others are characteristically Ayala's including those of education *(A.M.D.G.)* and vacillating personality (Alberto Díaz de Guzmán), and truly impart a transitional nature to *Prometheus* and other poematic novels.

Neither the chapters of *Sunday Sunlight* nor of *The Fall of the House of Limón* were headed by poems in their first version. The poems included in *Sunday Sunlight* are written in the traditional old ballad form, a concession to the verses taken from the *Cantar de Mio Cid (Epic of Mio Cid)* that serve as an anagram to the novel. The couplet "¡Quál ventura serie esta, si ploguiesse al Criador, / que assomasse essora el Çid Campeador!" ("How fortunate it would be, if God willed / That the Cid Campeador would appear now!") is taken from the poem's third part, "La afrenta de Corpes" ("The Effrontery of Corpes") after the Cid's two daughters are shamed and beaten while tied to oaks in the Corpes forest by their husbands, the Carrión noblemen. The echoes of *Sunday Sunlight* do not originate in ancient mythology, but rather in classical Spanish literature, not only the

Cid and *Romancero* but the honor plays of Lope de Vega and Calderón de la Barca and their modernization in the ballads of Antonio Machado.

Sunday Sunlight tells of two lovers from the town of Cenciella (as in *The Fox's Paw* and *Troteras y danzaderas*), the passive and gentle lawyer Cástor and the young and virginal Balbina. The novel begins as they plan for their April wedding one week later, when increasing signs of doom, underscored by the eight emblematic poems at the beginning of each chapter, foreshadow the tragedy that awaits them both. Owing to small-town political rivalries between the Becerriles (Calves) and the Chorizos (Sausages) parties, disputes of land ownership, and amorous rejections involving Joaco and his granddaughter Balbina, the young lovers are made to suffer. Undaunted and heedless of the repeated omens against their safety, Cástor and Balbina take walks in the Sunday sunlight, the brightest of all according to Cástor, an amateur painter of landscapes (like Alberto Díaz Guzmán and Ayala himself). The couple is surprised by seven of the Becerriles in the woods, and a scene parallel to "The Effrontery of Corpes" ensues as they tie Cástor to a tree and proceed in succession to rape his bride before his eyes. Loyal to Balbina, Cástor saves her from committing suicide and then marries her. Instead of seeking vengeance against the violators, the newlyweds, their child, and Balbina's grandfather decide to emigrate to America where their shame can be laid to rest, having failed to secure a peaceful existence even in the city of Pilares. Unfortunately, on the same vessel they meet several Cenciella neighbors who are aware of their plight and who also want to escape from the internecine warfare between the Becerriles and the Chorizos. The desperate couple perish together willingly ("se dejaron morir dulcemente")[17] when the ship capsizes during a storm.

Sunday Sunlight is one of the most emotionally charged pieces of fiction to come from Ayala's pen. In what may very well be the best narrative of the trilogy, Ayala ironically contrasts the introductory poetry of each chapter with the occurrences therein. For example, there is no modern Cid to avenge the rapes and no popular uprising in the manner of Lope's *Fuenteovejuna*. Instead, Cástor and his family flee the country, the people simply gossip, and Castille is damned as a poisoned land—much as in Machado's "La tierra de Alvargonzález" (The land of Alvargonzález). There exists an implicit condemnation in these verse-prose dislocations. Certainly in Ayala's mind is the decline of self-worth of the Spaniard and his society.

The basis for Ayala's third poematic novel, *The Fall of the House of Limón,* lies in a celebrated incident known as the crime of Don Benito, also re-created by Pío Baroja in his novel *Los visionarios* published in 1932. Divided into eleven short chapters with their corresponding poems, *The Fall of the House of Limón* is the longest and the most complicated novelette of the trilogy. It takes place at two different times—the present and the immediate past—and in two different locations—a Madrid boardinghouse and a manor house in Guadalfranco (Guadalajara). The opening and closing chapters are set in the present in the boardinghouse where two older female guests remain a mystery to the rest of the boarders. The main story line (excluding Ayala's digressions) concerns the powerful Limón clan, which autocratically dominates the province of Guadalfranco somewhere in western Spain. The fortunes of the Limones begin to sour as power passes from the founder to the daughter Fernanda. The family, reduced to the aging father, Fernanda, her sister Dominica, and her brother Arias, perilously maintains control of Guadalfranco while the citizenry increasingly resents Fernanda's authoritarianism. Each of the introductory poems strikes a more alarming note than the previous one. Yet, ephemerally, there seems to be a way to avoid a tragedy whose dimensions have grown with the passing of time. The ambitious lawyer Próspero Merlo wants to marry Dominica, a target for her brother's unnatural attentions, but fortuitously Arias himself falls in love with a girl he has seen in the street. Chords that echo Shakespeare's *Hamlet* ("love in the hands of a madman") in reference to Arias's pathological fixations[18] strike, and all is undone when Próspero is jailed for the murder of Arias's girl and her mother whom Próspero had secretly stabbed to death. Thus begins the fall of the house of Limón as the populace, anxious to rid itself of their yoke, cries for their ouster. When Arias confesses to the rape and murders so that Próspero may marry his sister, their tragedy draws to a close. Próspero refuses to marry Dominica on account of all that has transpired, and Arias and his servant and accomplice Bermudo (both medieval names that underscore the brutality of the crimes) are put to death. Fernanda and Dominica ultimately prove to be the two mysterious women dressed in mourning black at the Madrid boardinghouse—the level to which the Limón fortunes have fallen.

The Fall of the House of Limón, a novel of violent passions, owes a great deal of its interest to the plot itself as it develops in a play of opposites with the introductory poems and to the sharp deline- ation of characters—especially Arias whose emotional disturbances (jealous frenzies, cruelty, and impulsiveness)—make them rather unforgettable. Other than the social criticism of political bossism *(caciquismo),* this may be Ayala's most strictly literary narrative of the trilogy, unless some *engagée* character is suggested by the double entendre found in the title, *The Fall of the House of Limón,* versus "the falling of the lemons."

The Major Novels

In the five-year period dating from 1921 to 1926 Ayala wrote three novels that evince his mastery of the genre, mature works bringing him such international renown that even the *New York Times* reviewed them,[19] a notable exception for a Spanish novelist. In Spain he is ranked alongside Unamuno and Baroja. And yet, after 1926, Ramón Pérez de Ayala was never again to write another novel. These works, considered the zenith of his art as a novelist, are *Belarmino y Apolonio* (1921); *Honeymoon, Bittermoon* and its sequel, *The Trials of Urbano and Simona,* and *Tiger Juan* with its continuation, *El curandero de su honra.* The duality of the last two bipartite novels is reflected in the titles (twice over in *Honeymoon, Bittermoon),* in most of the main characters (Belarmino-Apolonio, Urbano-Simona, Tigre-Juan), in the novélistic-essayistic nature of the works, in their tragicomic tone, and finally in the complex duality that Ayala con- fers upon his heroes and heroines.

Belarmino y Apolonio begins in an old boardinghouse with some- one's tale of gossip. The speaker here, Don Amaranto de Fraile, a two-bit philosopher ("un Sócrates de tres pesetas") who has spent some forty-five years in boardinghouses, opines that the true Spanish university nowadays is really the boardinghouse—once again insin- uating the theme of learning through life versus learning through books so often explored by Ayala in previous novels. The narrator, while listening, recalls how in this very same boardinghouse he had also heard the story of the Limón family, a pointed remembrance that can further include *Tinieblas en las cumbres, The Fox's Paw,* and *Sunday Sunlight,* whose beginnings are similarly situated. As the characters become more individualized, the priest Don Guillén stands out from the rest. The son of the shoemaker Apolonio Caramanzana, Don Guillén has come to Madrid to deliver sermons during Holy Week. A likable personage, he appears in marked contrast to the earlier portrayals of the loathsome Jesuit priests of *A.M.D.G.* Ayala good-naturedly has Don Guillén eating meat during Lent because the canon regards it as an "artificial sin."

One evening in a café near the boardinghouse the narrator sees Angustias, a woman who, though she resembles a "Raphael virgin," not only turns out to be a prostitute called "La Pinta" but also the daughter of another shoemaker, Belarmino Pinta. With the two protagonists of the title thus alluded to, the narrative examines where exactly their lives were played out. Chapter 2, "Rúa Ruera, vista de dos lados" ("Ruera Street, Seen From Two Sides"), explores the dual perspectivism suggested in its caption. This main street of Pilares (again, Oviedo), where Belarmino and Apolonio each had his shoeshop on opposite sides, is viewed by Juan Lirio, the painter, and his friend Pedro Lario. The artist finds the mixed architecture and variety of houses utterly charming, whereas the positivist Spencerian philosophy of the latter makes him declare the Rúa Ruera unredeemably ugly. These dualities, resulting from physical contrasts or personal dialogues, form a complex net of dialectics that extends from one end of the novel to the other. Seven of the eight chapter headings announce it: chapter 1, "Don Guillén y la Pinta"; 2, "Rúa Ruera, vista de dos lados" ("Ruera Street, Seen From Two Sides"); 3, "Belarmino y su hija" ("Belarmino and His Daughter"); 4, "Apolonio y su hijo" ("Apolonio and His Son"); 5, "El filósofo y el dramaturgo" ("The Philosopher and the Dramatist"); 6, "El drama y la filosofía" ("Drama and Philosophy"—note the reversal of order of disciplines from the previous chapter); and 7, "Pedrito y Angustias" ("Petey and Angustias").

The narrative, strictly speaking, begins in chapter 3, "Belarmino and His Daughter." Belarmino, the philosopher-shoemaker—always badgered by his wife, hounded by creditors, and importuned by customers—is given to daydreaming and consulting the dictionary, a book he believes contains all the knowledge in the universe since it lists all of the words in the language. Belarmino invariably converses in a newfangled speech of his own creation; Apolonio, in contrast, speaks in verse most of the time. The greatest joy in Belarmino's life is the little girl Angustias whom he has loved as a daughter since infancy, though she is really an orphaned niece, the

daughter of his dead sister. The name of Belarmino's wife, Xuan-
tipa—Xuana la Tipa ("Jane Doe")—derives from that of Socrates'
wife, Xantippe, thus reflecting his philosophical outlook on life.

Belarmino's tranquil existence is shaken when another shoemaker,
Apolonio, comes to Pilares and opens a modern repair shop across
the street from Belarmino's. Knowing the latter's indigent situation
and his penchant for much philosophizing and little laboring, the
townspeople foresee Belarmino's commercial collapse. Apolonio's
shop, financed by a small inheritance, puts Belarmino out of business
in no time. The competition and the mounting debts persuade his
creditor, a usurer named Bellido, to close him down, but not before
Apolonio's son (Guillén) and Belarmino's daughter (Angustias) fall
in love. Following the loss of his shop, Belarmino, through the
intercession of the Dominican monks, is allowed a tiny stall in the
entranceway—below street level—of the palace belonging to
the Marqués de San Madrigal. In the new locale Belarmino continues
his ways and is now completely happy since he pays no rent, his
wife is forbidden from entering his little shop, and Angustias keeps
doting on him. His philosophizing earns Belarmino an ever-wid-
ening audience of university students (i.e., life versus books), among
them the colorful Froilán Escobar, nicknamed "Alligator" for his
lethargic ways.

Apolonio, though victorious on the commercial front, cannot
overcome his jealousy of his rival's popularity. He seeks fame by
persuading an influential friend, the old man Novillo (irony:
"youngish" or "calf"), to produce a play he has written. Novillo,
who visits Apolonio's shop in order to watch the spinster Felicita
la Quemada ("burned out"), who is secretly in love with him, pass
by every day, agrees to Apolonio's proposal. The play is staged, not
as a drama but as a farce, with tremendous success—an outcome
that leads Apolonio to begin neglecting his shop. Unfortunately for
him, a merchant comes to Pilares selling ready-made shoes, and
Apolonio's business falters. Further misfortunes befall him when he
is apprised in a letter from his son that Guillén and Angustias are
going to elope. Despite the pleas of the young couple along with
those of the bishop and the Dominicans, enough pressure is put on
the lovers so that their marriage does not take place. Guillén—then
called Pedrito—is cajoled into the priesthood, and Angustias, ban-
ished from her own home by Xantipa, disappears. Felicitas's and
Novillo's love affair likewise fails when he dies from pneumonia.

All of these events leave Belarmino disconsolate. Overcome with disillusionment, he gives up both shoemaking and philosophy. Belarmino has reached a point of self-realization, whereby he sees futility in both the practical and the metaphysical. Now a widower, he seeks refuge in a retirement home, withdrawing from life and those who thought him a fool. There Belarmino is soon joined by the usurer Bellido who drove him to ruin and also by Apolonio whom his son Guillén, by then an important canon, had interned there, being unable to control either his financial or sexual excesses. The two rivals reconcile their differences after Apolonio, boastful of being rich, is secretly observed filling his Vichy water bottle from a fountain. Silently watching Apolonio, Belarmino hesitates as to whether he should denounce him to the community and be forever his victor or not. Belarmino decides against it, and the two embrace, declaring to one another that they are in truth the other's half. On this Easter Sunday when Belarmino and Apolonio make peace with each other, the narrator brings the prostitute Angustias to Guillén, now a priest. Their love, transformed necessarily into friendship, promises to be as genuine and lasting as their fathers'. Christian love, it seems, has solved the problems of them all on this Holy day.

Belarmino y Apolonio's narrative structure is not lineal, but a complex arrangement of occurrences seen from several points of view, regardless of chronology or internal order, so that the reader confronts the same scene from different vantage points. There are three narrators: (1) the first person who witnesses the action of the boardinghouse between Tuesday and Sunday of Holy Week; (2) an omniscient narrator who tells of the happenings of Pilares during several years; and (3) the priest Don Guillén who soliloquizes in chapters 4 and 7. Consequently, almost all of the characters are seen from more than one vantage point, episodes are interwoven back and forth, and time becomes elasticized as erstwhile children seen in the present are older than their parents whose story we learn in the middle of the novel. Many essayistic and lyrical digressions deal with a wide variety of themes (boardinghouses in different countries, poetry commentaries, the role of the middle classes), but *Belarmino y Apolonio*'s main themes are greater than these. They address the value of language and communication, the contrasting duality of man, the equally truthful manifold facets of reality (perspectivism), and the worth of Christian love in the end. At age forty, when the novel was published, Ayala's anticlerical religious outlook certainly had changed from the earlier period of *A.M.D.G.*: the Dominicans provide Belarmino with a new shop, the bishop does not cave in to the duchess's demand that he refuse to marry Angustias and Guillén, Guillén as a priest provides for his father and for Angustias and her father later on, Guillén's love metamorphoses from eros to agape, and the Easter rejoicing coincides with the characters' own. All of this may explain why *A.M.D.G.* had no further editions after its initial publication while its author was alive and why he excluded it from his *Obras Completas*.

Honeymoon, Bittermoon and *The Trials of Urbano and Simona* constitute one single work, separate in title but indivisible in concept. It certainly makes no sense to read either one without the other, as may be deduced from the four internal divisions the author provided: "Cuarto Menguante" ("Waning Moon"), "Cuarto creciente" ("Crescent Moon"), "Novilunio" ("New Moon"), and "Plenilunio" ("Full Moon"). The first two correspond to *Honeymoon, Bittermoon* and the last two to *The Trials of Urbano and Simona*. Both works were completed within one month of each other—September and October 1922, respectively. In their last critical edition they were issued as one volume under the title of *The Novels of Urbano and Simona*.[20]

The first volume introduces the main characters. On the one side are Doña Micaela and Don Leoncio, the strong-willed mother and weak father of the young and innocent Urbano, who still lives at home with his preceptor Don Cástulo. On the other side, there is the old Doña Rosita, her widowed daughter Doña Victoria, whose husband's gambling debts have ruined the family and mortgaged all of their properties, and the granddaughter Simona, as young and guileless as Urbano. Don Leoncio opposes the marriage of his son Urbano, but Doña Micaela insists on seeing it through because she covets Simona's apparent wealth and relishes the young couple's innocence. The marriage does take place because Urbano and Simona have loved each other since early childhood, but since neither one is sexually mature their union is not consummated. Once the characters have been introduced and the stage set under the slow tempo of the "Waning Moon" segment, the "Crescent Moon" begins. Doña Micaela, aware of a lack of consummation, rushes to separate the couple when creditors rain down upon Doña Victoria's country estate and take it over in lieu of payments. She wants a divorce for her son. Before Doña Rosita dies from the shock, she passes on to her granddaughter Simona all of her jewels and tells her not to give up on Urbano. Meanwhile, Don Leoncio, also bankrupt, tries to take his own life as his wife rushes to his side to prevent further suicide attempts.

This fable of innocent young love, reminiscent of Daphnis and Chloe, contrasts sharply with the earthier and more carnal relationship begun between Cástulo, Urbano's preceptor, and Conchona (corruption of *cachonda*, i.e., "aroused"), Simona's maid. Further classical references are suggested by the title *The Trials of Urbano and Simona* which point to the mythical trials (i.e., "labors") of Hercules. Urbano and Simona too must endure suffering, privation, and time spent away from each other in order to reap the benefits of marital bliss.[21] "New Moon" continues the story of the unfortunate lovers and their luckier counterparts. Cástulo and Conchona marry, set up an academy for higher studies, and are happier with each passing day, thus proving that learned knowledge (the bookish Cástulo) and natural experience (Conchona) are not mutually exclusive. Doña Victoria, absent more and more frequently with a priest friend of hers, takes Simona to live with her seven spinster sisters. Urbano, now a teacher in Cástulo's academy, wishes to see his bride and through several deceitful tricks succeeds not only in seeing her but in consummating their marriage. When their rendezvous is discovered, Simona is placed in a convent from where Urbano abducts her and together they go in search of freedom.

The Novels of Urbano and Simona constitute a new twist on the bildungsroman archetype. Here a man and a woman come into a marriage as children and are forced to grow intellectually, emotionally, and sexually before they can live as man and wife. Simona's dedication, fidelity, and suffering lead her to this plateau; Urbano's determination, upbringing, and faith carry him to his. An inadequate education, both institutional and familial—perhaps Ayala's most lasting leitmotiv—almost wrecked their lives, as love and sex are themes that Ayala explores fully and artistically.

Love continues to be the main theme of Ayala's next novel, *Tiger Juan,* as well as of *El curandero de su honra,* the last one he wrote and published, and for which he received Spain's National Prize for Literature. The two titles, issued in separate volumes, cannot be understood separately. Like the preceeding works, the two must be considered as one, an indication Ayala reiterates as each volume is divided into musically titled sections that reflect the narrative tempo:

Tiger Juan into "Adagio" and "Presto," and *El curandero de su honra* into "Presto," "Adagio," "Coda," and "Parergon."

Tiger Juan's setting is the by-now-familiar town of Pilares. Here the action takes place in the market square with special attention focused on Juan Guerra Madrigal's small stand and those of his neighbors Doña Iluminada and Doña Marica. This fierce-looking man nicknamed Tiger Juan dispenses medical advice and herbal potions, and writes letters and wills on the side. He has been named Tiger Juan for his Calderonian belief in a man's honor, which may have indirectly resulted in the loss of his wife when she hid the lover of the wife of Juan's superior officer in her own bedroom. Tiger Juan, thinking he had been dishonored, almost choked her to death but subsequently relented, convinced of her virtue. Though she recovered temporarily, she eventually died, and he felt responsible ever after. Since then Tiger Juan, nothing less than a ferocious misogynist, has been living as a widower with his nephew Colás, a bastard whom he has raised from earliest childhood and who now is finishing his law studies. Juan is befriended by two men, Nachín de Nacha, who comes to town on the market days—Thursdays and Sundays—to peddle hunting caps, and by Vespasiano Cebón, a traveling salesman who claims to be successful with many women. Juan envies Vespasiano's dominance over females whom he himself blames for all of the world's ills, with the exception of his neighbors Doña Marica and Doña Iluminada; the latter, a widow, is secretly in love with Tiger Juan who, of course, remains oblivious to her sentiments.

Colás loves Doña Marica's granddaughter Herminia, but she rejects him because of her fear of living anywhere near Tiger Juan and also because she believes she loves Vespasiano. Upon her rejection, Colás joins the army and goes away, abandoning both his uncle and his studies. Both actions further fuel Tiger Juan's hatred of women—that is, until one evening when he goes to play cards at Doña Marica's and notices Herminia for the first time. He is struck by the likeness of the young woman to his deceased wife. Tiger Juan eventually believes Herminia to be the reincarnation of Engracia and falls in love with her. Although convinced of his honorable intentions, Herminia rejects her grandmother's advice to marry Tiger Juan; she is afraid of him, even if she is drawn to him by his strength and courage.

Finally in *El curandero de su honra,* Herminia, in spite of her misgivings regarding Tiger Juan and her lingering attraction for Vespasiano, becomes engaged to the former. When Vespasiano comes to Pilares shortly before the wedding and sees Herminia, he behaves like the archetypal Don Juan, making advances but no commitments, and leaves her to wait for the marriage to take place. At this juncture, Tiger Juan portrays the dishonored husband who kills his wife in Calderón's play, *El médico de su honra* (The physician [note the irony of the title] of his honor), a role he carries off with a vengeance to the loud approval of the townspeople. Notice has been served on Herminia, and the ceremony ensues. On Vespasiano's next visit Herminia flees with him, but nothing happens between them. There is no adultery; nevertheless, Tiger Juan's honor has been besmirched. Partly on Vespasiano's advice (he wants no burdens or responsibilities and, like every Don Juan, is incapable of love) and partly forced into it by Colás, his girl friend Carmina, and Doña Iluminada, Herminia returns home very ill. After a night of despair on his saint's day—San Juan, traditionally a night for lovers—Tiger Juan and his wife reconcile silently; but, feeling dishonored, he slits open his veins. Herminia, who now realizes the meaning and worth of love, stops Tiger Juan from killing himself.

In the "Coda" the two have a son and live happily. Vespasiano proves to be a false friend and only half the man that Tiger Juan is. The novel's two main themes, love and honor, must exist side by side. Neither is outdated, and one cannot exist without the other in a marriage. The stereotypical Don Juan along with the rhetorical honor previously espoused by Tiger Juan are discarded as worthless obstacles to happiness. Love as one passion and honor as another complement each other in the life of Tiger Juan, a man whose contrasting last names Juan Guerra (War) and Madrigal (Love song) characterize him and summarize the novel perfectly.

Ramón Perez de Ayala's novels are the most serious and difficult examples of this genre in the first half of the twentieth century in Spain. Unlike those of Unamuno, with whom he has been compared, Ayala's novels fit into a more traditional mold. Ayala does not write "problem novels" or "limit-situation novels" as did Unamuno. Nor is his fiction action- or entertainment-oriented as is Baroja's. Neither are his narratives similar to Valle's period *(Sonatas)* or reformist *(The Tyrant)* works. Ayala's novels posit an intellectual challenge to readers on several fronts: they are concerned with the structure and basis of the novelistic genre itself *(Belarmino y Apolonio)*, they explore the transformation of the autobiographical into the universal (the four Alberto Díaz de Guzmán works), they re-create and update ancient mythology *(Prometheus)* or classical Spanish literature *(Tiger Juan, El curandero de su honra)*, they are as timeless in their themes as they are universal (education, man's behavior and self, passion, communication, art) and, finally, they elevate language to an almost rarefied level that combines the use of colloquialisms and profanity with a learned, almost elitist vocabulary.

Chapter Six
Gabriel Miró:
The Impressionist Novel

Gabriel Miró Ferrer, another member of the Generation of 1914, felt little kinship with his literary contemporaries. Miró elected to pursue the kind of literature that disavows political or social reform. His fiction stands on its own artistic worth, unencumbered by idealism of any sort. Like Ayala, a lawyer, a nascent painter, and a product of a Jesuit education, Miró allowed his aesthetic sensitivity to turn him away from the intellectualized prose that emanated from Pérez de Ayala's pen, producing instead an impressionist and lyrical fiction in whose perfection may lie its greatest peril. Upon reading one of Miró's most controversial novels, El obispo leproso (The leper bishop), Ortega complained of the "impeccable and implacable" perfection of a prose whose "largest defect is its excessive quality."[1] The charge of being a difficult writer has stuck since Ortega made that statement in 1927, with the result that Miró's readership, small up to that date, remains limited to a select public and a few scholars.

Miró's Biobibliography

Gabriel Miró died at his home on the Paseo del Prado in Madrid on Tuesday, 27 May, 1930 at nine-thirty in the evening as a result of postoperative complications following an appendectomy. He was fifty years old at the time. His personal biography can be summed up briefly and hardly merits recollection unless his vocation as an author is taken into account. Miró himself was not at all unhappy at finding that he had no biographer while he was alive.[2] He was born to Juan Miró Moltó and Encarnación Ferrer Ons on 28 July, 1879 in the Mediterranean port city of Alicante where his father was the chief engineer of the port authority. This second child of a very Catholic marriage—Don Juan had studied for the priesthood—was sent at age eight to the nearby Jesuit college in Orihuela. A boarder at the Colegio de Santo Domingo for five years, the young

and impressionable Gabriel did not fare very well and spent long
periods of illness in the school's infirmary through whose windows
he contemplated his first "melancholy aesthetics" as he labeled the
many sunsets viewed from his sickbed.[3] The austere climate of these
times is later recalled in several chapters of *Libro de Sigüenza* (The
Book of Sigüenza). At Santo Domingo de Orihuela when he was
ten, Miró wrote his first remembered literary piece, the essay "Un
día de campo" (A day outdoors) describing an outing into the country, for which he received a silver medal. Proud of the merit acknowledged the adolescent Miró's vainglory was rebuked by the
Jesuits who told him that the prize had been awarded mistakenly.

Gabriel spent his high-school years back with his family in Alicante while he studied at the local "instituto." His secondary education behind him, Miró enrolled in the law college at the University
of Valencia. For reasons that are unclear, perhaps because he found
the course work too difficult at Valencia, Miró switched to the
University of Granada, then back to Valencia, and finally graduated
from Granada in 1900. He received no further formal instruction.
The remaining part of his education is almost entirely autodidactic,
not all of it coming from books. Miró learned to exercise his artistic
sensitivity and to master a sense of color, proportion, and visual
acuity from his uncle, Lorenzo Casanova, a painter of veritable talent
who was just as fond of reading as he was of working with oils.
The young Miró was a constant visitor in Casanova's studio until
the man died in 1900, having done three portraits of Gabriel who
wondered if he would not have become a painter himself had his
mentor not died.[4] What was not learned at the studio, Miró found
on the shelves of his father's library. Don Juan, aside from collecting
the scientific books pertaining to his profession, owned volumes on
travel, history, and romantic literature as well as the classics—
among them the *Divine Comedy, Don Quixote,* and the Bible. Miró
much preferred these works to school texts, which he always looked
upon with indifference.

He finished his degree in law with some difficulty due to a lack
of interest in the subject. His choice of a career in jurisprudence
was probably motivated by the feeling that it would afford him a
comfortable living with plenty of free time to devote to other pursuits in the arts, either literature or painting. Miró tried twice to
secure a judgeship but failed both times, a painful disappointment
recorded in *Libro de Sigüenza.* These frustrated attempts, which in-

deed would have permitted him to enjoy the kind of existence he envisioned, meant that his life was never too far from economic worries, having made up his mind to hold literature as his most important occupation. It is fair to say, however, that he was insufficiently prepared to earn such a position by competitive examination. As the surveys of Miró's library done by R. Vidal, E. L. King, and I. R. Macdonald attest, he had next to nothing in the way of law books, most of the space being occupied by classics and religious works, very few of which belonged to his contemporaries.[5]

Miró's initial published writings appeared in the bimonthly *El Ibero*. For a period of four years Miró's short stories were featured in this Alicantine journal, the first of which, "Del natural" (From nature) appeared on 1 March, 1902. Publishing excerpts or even advance segments of his books in newspapers and magazines was a habit Miró never lost, mainly for economic reasons. In time the most prestigious periodicals, among them Barcelona's *La Vanguardia* and *La Publicidad*, Madrid's *El Sol*, *El Imparcial*, and *La Gaceta Literaria*, and Buenos Aires's *La Nación*, all demanded his pages.

At twenty Miró wrote "a volume of articles; on one of which [he] dwelt so long that it became a book: *La mujer de Ojeda* [Ojeda's wife], 1900."[6] He so much regretted having written it that, together with *Hilván de Escenas* (A series of scenes), it was repudiated when the time came to compile the editions of his complete works. Neither one has been reissued, and the same fate befell *El hijo santo* (The holy son), dating from 1909, the *Del huerto provinciano* (The country orchard), which appeared in 1912. During these years Miró also wrote *Del vivir* (About living), published in 1904, *La novela de mi amigo* (My friend's novel) in 1908, and the novelette *Nómada* (Nomad) issued the same day on which Miró's father died. This last work was awarded a first prize by the magazine *El cuento semanal*. While the jury, made up of Pío Baroja, Valle Inclán, and Felipe Trigo, lent the award some degree of merit, it also meant for its recipient a modest amount of notoriety since notice of the prize and a picture of Miró were carried by almost all of the Madrid papers. The publicity probably influenced the local government of his native Alicante to take notice of his growing stature and appoint him to a more lucrative bureaucratic post, a sinecure which, in addition to an increased salary, freed Miró to write.

Las cerezas del cementerio (The graveyard cherries, 1910), a long novel still imbued with romantic and decadent overtones and motifs, opens the middle stage of Miró's literary production. Now married and father of two daughters, Miró moved his family to Barcelona, a city in whose newspapers he had been collaborating and where he had found employment with the publisher Vecchi y Ramos as editor of a planned Catholic encyclopedia. For fourteen months Miró slaved over the project, coordinating work, researching materials, interviewing some theologians and corresponding with others, all of which left him little time for his own creative work. Nevertheless, the chores were to his liking on the whole and he devoted himself willingly to the tasks at hand. Unfortunately, with the outbreak of World War I, Vecchi y Ramos went bankrupt and the encyclopedia was never published, nor was Miró adequately compensated for the many months of labor which, to the detriment of his own work, he had invested. Also around 1915, Barcelona felt the scourge of a typhoid epidemic to which his oldest daughter, Clemencia, fell prey. Miró, completely destitute and grief-stricken at the likelihood of losing his child, must have considered those days as the darkest hour of his life. The danger passed, however, and as an act of thanksgiving he wrote a small play, really an *auto sacramental* (a short, religious, and symbolic play) "La cieguecita de Belen" (The blind girl from Bethlehem), together with the composer Enrique Granados, who wrote the music for it, since his children had also been stricken with the malady. The piece remains unpublished, neither family consenting to its dissemination, though it was staged by the Miró and the Granados children plus those of Dr. Pi Suñer in the Christmas season of 1915.[7]

The year and a half of work on the encyclopedia was, happily, not in vain. From knowledge acquired during the project, Miró drew the sources for his most controversial and least understood book, the one that made him famous. Titled *Figuras de la Pasión del Señor (Figures of the Passion of our Lord)* and published in two volumes in 1916 and 1917, it was received with skepticism and eventually denounced as unorthodox vis-á-vis Catholic hagiography. The largely aesthetic interpretation of Biblical themes and figures brought Miró much distress: the jailing of Valdés Prida, editor of the Gijón newspaper *El Noroeste,* for running a chapter of the book on 6 April, 1917, Good Friday; his own exclusion from the Spanish Royal Academy even though he was sponsored by Azorín, Ricardo León (1877–1943), and Armando Palacio Valdés (1853–1938); and denial of the Fastenrath Prize sponsored by the Royal Academy on two separate occasions.[8]

In 1919, at about the same time, Miró wrote *El humo dormido* (The slumbering smoke), a book of poetical narrative essays, fictional but seminally autobiographical, difficult to read because of its density and slow narrative tempo. *El abuelo del rey* (The grandfather of the king, 1915), and *Libro de Sigüenza* also date from this period. The latter includes most of the essays and stories whose protagonist is the same "Sigüenza" encountered in *Del vivir*. This constitutes Miró's middle period, a stage of affirmation of values, style, and narrative technique.

At the age of forty, Miró, unable to secure suitable employment in Barcelona, pulled up stakes once again and headed for Madrid in July of 1920. There in the nation's capital, where he was to live the remaining ten years of his life, Prime Minister Antonio Maura, an admirer of Miró, appointed the writer to a relatively well-remunerated bureaucratic post. This position did much to alleviate his financial strain because even if it did not quite suffice to support his whole family—Gabriel's mother and his daughters lived with the family—the sales of his books, the contract to have his complete works published by Biblioteca Nueva, and some translations he did from French and Catalan together made their living reasonably comfortable.

The books done in this last decade are the purest from an aesthetic vantage point. These are works on which Miró labored slowly and devotedly, carefully distilling his narrative resources until successfully producing an elliptical, pure, poetic prose. In his forties Miró published only three novels: *Nuestro Padre San Daniel* (Our father San Daniel, 1921), *El obispo leproso* (The leper bishop, 1926), and *Años y leguas* (The years and the leagues, 1928), though strictly speaking the first two are really one book since both share the same literary microcosm and must be regarded as a bipartite novel. It is true that in 1922 he had also published *Niño y grande* (Young and old), but this work is an amplified version of his earlier *Amores de Antón Hernando* (The loves of Antón Hernando, 1909).

If this last stage of Miró's life does not seem prolific, at least it brought the writer more peace than years past. The "Mariano de Cavia" prize awarded by the prestigious daily *ABC* for his "Huerto de Cruces" (Cross orchard) chapter of *Años y leguas* must have helped ease the slights done him by the Royal Academy. A resigned and

serene tone characterizes the entire breadth of the works truly belonging to this third stage of Miró's life as an author, a fitting close
for the even-tempered fiction of this transcendent novelist.

Aesthetics and Classification of Miró's Works

Miró's work constituted, to a great extent, his life. He re-created
in his pages childhood, adolescence, youth, and maturity. Miró the
writer never forgot nor ever let go of Miró the man. His art is so
subjective that it includes the greater part of himself. This close
relationship between the two has as the only obstacle to a total
identification what is known as aesthetic distance, that transub-
stantiation which transforms daily reality into universal art forms.
When in an interview a newsman asked Miró what literature meant
to him, Miró replied: "The same thing as life: serenity and simplicity. . . . Each writer must mirror in his style the norms of his
life."[9]

In his twenties Miró forged his intellectual and artistic founda-
tions. It was a time of trial and error, of indecision, and of rethinking
the components that ultimately constituted his aesthetic mode. During the decade from 1900 to 1910 Miró chose to become a writer
and abandoned all pretense of a career in law. He saw one of his
works, *Nómada* (1908), win an important literary prize, and he
attained sufficient aesthetic criteria to repudiate four of his earliest
pieces. It was also the time of the character Sigüenza's initial appearance, that enigmatic alter ego whose lifespan parallels Miró's
own in the book *Del vivir*. These initial works—*La mujer de Ojeda,
Hilván de escenas, Del vivir, La novela de mi amigo, Nómada, Del huerto
provinciano, Corpus y otros cuentos, La palma rota, El hijo santo,* and
Amores de Antón Hernando—betray a slight romanticism. All of them
are brief and written in a style which has yet to crystallize in Miró's
later "decir por insinuación" (telling by insinuating). Some, especially *Del vivir,* bear the burden of too many classical allusions which
break up the gentle flow of his prose.

Las cerezas del cementerio, Miró's first full-length novel, initiates a
second decade in his literary career where Miró's lyrical and impressionistic style no longer rises and falls but instead becomes one
of the strongest attributes of his art as an even, poetic, and cultivated
prose. The years from 1910 to 1921 saw the publication not only
of *Las cerezas del cementerio* but also of the novels *Niño y grande, El*

abuelo del rey, Libro de Sigüenza, El humo dormido, and the two volumes of the *Figures of the Passion of our Lord* in addition to one collection of short stories *El angel, El molino, El caracol del faro* (The angel, The windmill, The conch at the lighthouse). These were the works, some of them true masterpieces, that established Miró as a respected author who had to contend with the envy of those lesser than he. It was a stage of great creative impetus, whose books were long and ambitious in scope, achieved, mostly under trying personal circumstances, through considerable artistic efforts in order to overcome hosts of antagonistic critics as well as those others whose applause needed to be discounted for lack of scholarly rigor.

The two novels of the last decade, *Our Father San Daniel* and its continuation, *El obispo leproso,* and the third Sigüenza book, *Años y leguas,* are the culmination of Miró's narrative art. In the latter the author may have foreseen the finality of these works when he wrote in its closing paragraph "Y aquí dejaré a Sigüenza, quizá para siempre . . ." (And here I shall leave Sigüenza, perhaps forever . . .) two years prior to his own death.[10]

Upon enumerating the most salient notes of Miró's production— synaesthesia, extreme subjectivism, fragmentary structures, static narratives, masses of color and sensations, abundance of pathetic fallacy, hyperesthesia—it becomes obvious that most if not all of them coincide with a description of impressionism, the school of painting whose name derives from the Frenchman Edouard Manet's (1832–1883) canvas *Impressions.* Miró neither analyzes nor explains; he merely details his own emotions received as impressions upon the contemplation of a subject. Miró's impressionism turns out to be a reflection of a given reality, experienced through the emotional gamut of his own individual sensitivity. Such subjectivism confers upon the impressionist microcosm—anthropocentric by antonomasia—a personal interpretation that many may find difficult to share. There are few highlights or climaxes in an impressionist narrative of this sort; its tone is always one of uniformity and apathy. With the lack of narrative crescendos, it follows that there are no catharses either. Impressionism, Miró's brand in particular, makes any given reality totally dependent upon the sensitivity of the narrator since only through his perceptions, impressions, or sensations can all of what the reader has before him be revealed. Consequently Miró's style, especially his syntax, can be in many instances full of ellipses; his plots are inevitably weak and lacking in interest; his backgrounds are sensual, almost overpowering as sensations accumulate without any apparent order. Because Miró substitutes sensitivity for inspiration, impressions become the most important facet of his fiction; more than the object alluded to by the narrator, he is interested in the effect that particular object has had on the narrator himself. Overriding importance is given to the impressions caused by objects rather than the subjects themselves. Sensations and sentiments reveal Miró's fictional reality. They are the only complete facet of his art.

The First Works

The decade 1900–1910 saw the publication of Miró's first book-length narratives. *La mujer de Ojeda* appeared in 1901, *Hilván de escenas* in 1903, *Del vivir* in 1904, *Nómada* and *La novela de mi amigo* in 1908, *Amores de Antón Hernando* and *El hijo santo* in 1909, and *Las cerezas del cementerio* in 1910.

Except for *Las cerezas del cementerio,* all of these novels are brief and exhibit Miró's detectable penchant for the later themes of alienation, a pantheistic concept of nature, and a hypersensitivity on the part of the protagonists that invariably causes them to suffer. The first two works, *La mujer de Ojeda* and *Hilván de escenas,* as well as *El hijo santo,* later repudiated by the author, are today impossible to find since none of the three ever went past a first edition. All have been excluded from Miró's *Obras completas.* Miró himself declared that *La mujer de Ojeda* had brought him "muchos remordimientos artísticos" (many artistic regrets).[11] Juan Chabás, in his *Literatura española contemporánea,* summarizes its plot as a passionate love story whose characters are poorly drawn and whose style is somewhat careless.[12] The title of the second work, *Hilván de escenas,* can only point to the fragmentary structure of this book, equally dismissed by its author from further publications. As it stands, then, *Obras completas,* edited with a preface by Miró's daughter Clemencia—herself a poet—places *Del vivir* as the novelist's inaugural work. *Amores de Antón Hernando* is suppressed, appearing instead in a longer revised version retitled *Niño y grande* with the date 1922.

Nómada, the briefest of all of the first period novels, appeared initially in the pages of a well-known Madrid literary magazine, *El cuento semanal,* on 6 March, 1908 and received the publication's first prize. Though modest, this award did several things for the young author: it encouraged him to keep writing; it gave his name exposure outside his native city of Alicante; it aided him financially; and it helped him overcome his grief at the death of his father Don Juan Miró. *Nómada* tells of the undoing of the life of a just, rich, and powerful man named Diego from the town of Jijona in the province of Alicante. His life's misfortunes begin at the death of his wife and only daughter from an epidemic of typhoid fever. Disconsolate, Diego finds no refuge in the company of either his older sister Elvira, an embittered spinster, or the insensitive housemaid Virtudes. Consequently, he gives himself over to the low life of gambling and prostitutes until financially indigent, then leaves Jijona on a pilgrimage that takes him through southern Europe where, finding no balm for his broken heart, he is forced to beg for his food. Tired, ill, and disoriented, Diego returns to Alicante to expiate his sins, but again finds no peace even in his own house.

La novela de mi amigo has a parallel design. Federico Urrios, its protagonist and the friend of the narrator, is another failed individual whose life ends by his own hand. Urrios, a painter—the novel is dedicated to Miró's uncle and painter Lorenzo Casanova—feels his life take turn after turn for the worse while he remains helpless to control the events. Urrios' lack of will may be inspired by the Generation of 1898's concept of *abulia*. On the other hand, his demise is also the result of his own excessive artistic sensitivity, which renders him incapable of action. Federico lives in Madrid, making himself and others believe that he is on the verge of being discovered as a great artist. In this bohemian existence he meets a woman whom he marries, believing her to be a good prospect— the same reason that she has for marrying Federico. Having deceived his own mother regarding a prosperous future awaiting him in the world of art, the deceiver is now himself deceived by his wife. Lacking the financial means to sustain an existence in Madrid, they move to a town in the provinces where their life mires down in petty occurrences and privations of every sort. As each finds himself and herself cheated by the other, a sense of alienation between them grows to unbearable proportions. The birth of a daughter does little to alleviate the tension in the Urrios' household. The child eventually falls gravely ill with tuberculosis, an occasion that recalls to her father's mind the death of his own sister when as children the two had been playing and she burned herself so severely that she died. Now, with the death of his daughter, Federico realizes that he has no one or nothing left to live for. One night he simply walks into the sea and, sinking among the waves, perishes.

Both *Nómada* and *La novela de mi amigo* are pessimistic tales whose heroes are powerless to act, sensitive to an extreme, and unable to find in nature or their fellowmen the compassion needed to overcome their grief. Don Diego and Federico Urrios are pathetic human beings for whom life's realities are too much to handle. Their strength lies in their sensitive characters, in their love of nature, and in their appreciation of art's beauty. When confronted with the starker aspects of reality they cannot cope. In this decadentist vein Miró also produces his most significant character, his alter ego, Sigüenza.

Similar in its slow narrative tempo and doomed hero to these two initial pieces is Miró's first full-length novel, *Las cerezas del cementerio*. Published in 1910, the work marks the end of Miró's fictional apprenticeship and his beginning as a full-fledged novelist. It is a first major undertaking that fails in as many regards as it succeeds in others; in all of them, however, it reveals most of Miró's future characteristics as a novelist. *Las cerezas del cementerio* constitutes a polished work, well received at the time of its publication in spite of a mutilated first edition.

A semierotic, sensuous but anguished love between a young engineer, Félix, who suffers from a heart ailment, and a married woman, Beatriz, is the narrative thread woven by the author around themes that will become leitmotivs in nearly all of Miró's mature works: the unattainability of joy, the suffering on the part of the sensitive and the weak, and the sensual and disturbing role of nature. Set in the country during the summer where Félix (meaning "happy") and Beatriz (a reference to Dante's beloved) are vacationing, the novel slowly unfolds in a confusion of sensations (synesthesia)— particularly visual, gustatory, and olfactory. Nature takes on the role of another character as it conditions the behavior of Félix, Beatriz, and her daughter Julia. Literally and figuratively ill from his heart, Félix embodies anew the weak, decadent, will-less hero already seen in Miró's fiction. He is destined to fail and to die for reasons beyond his power to control.

Sensitivity, love, knowledge, and good breeding do not suffice when the challenges of reality have to be answered. Others are made to suffer alongside the hero because they too cannot cope or defend themselves. The cruelty to those who are crippled, even to animals, that so exacerbates the pathos of the narrative coexists in Miró's fiction alongside the admiration for exquisite beauty.

Las cerezas del cementerio is a stylistic triumph, which together with the many biblical and classical references brings the novel close to a prose poem. Miró's extraordinary vocabulary, his virtuosity in producing the exact word, and the impressionist technique used to portray a character or depict a scene lend *Las cerezas del cementerio* a fullness difficult to dispel. Perhaps too literary in concept, the novel manages to succeed in conveying—if not a believable microcosm— an unforgettable effect on the senses and the emotions of the reader. It conjures up a single vision of a romantic and decadentist canvas in which characters and background at times blur into one. The lack of a clear, strong plot—little happens—the slow tempo, the lushness of the setting, and the light of the season no doubt contribute to this impression.

The Autobiographical Works

Miró's novels lie at the limit of the genre, on the verge of being classified merely as what is vaguely labeled fiction. Modern novels tend to be more descriptive and less narrative, and to present a disconnected world rather than a perfectly ordered series of events. Miró's works exist within that disintegrating evolution of the genre. Action and plot are eschewed in favor of an intimate, confessional literature; in fact, such is the new novelistic outlook. The aesthetics influencing the key works in Miró's developing novelistic output derive from the character novel, the romance (introverted and personal narrative), the autobiography (introverted and intellectual narrative), and the confession (spiritual account).[13] Unequally assimilated, these four related types of narration produce three works that are typical of the totality of Miró's writings: *Del vivir* (1904), the first unrepudiated work; *Libro de Sigüenza* (1917), meridian work of his production; and *Años y leguas* (1928), the last work published in his lifetime. The three are characterized by a diffuse novelistic background befitting the journey—*homo viator* (man as a wanderer through life)—as well as similar structures, themes, and the presence of a common protagonist.

In *Del vivir, Libro de Sigüenza,* and *Años y leguas* the hero coincides with the author and occupies most of his attention; an introverted figure wounded by a certain weltanschauung (world weariness), he is extremely individualistic, and of an unmistakable personality. Sigüenza dominates the scenario of this history so completely that at times he appears to be its sole character.

Since Sigüenza coexisted with Miró, the books in which the character appears as the protagonist constitute landmarks by which Miró's production is measured. Like Don Quixote and Cervantes whose ages were quite close, Sigüenza and Miró may also have been the same age. Miró in 1904, date of publication of *Del vivir,* was twenty-five years old, when *Años y leguas* came out, forty-nine. Sigüenza's age, upon his return to the lands of his birth in the latter book, is over forty. The correspondence may not be exact, but the parallel suffices. Within the works themselves, autobiographical segments abound: the Jesuit college of Santo Domingo (572),[14] the examinations for judgeship (576), the presence of Miró's family— wife, daughters and older parents—(569), the wish for a few free hours in which to write (1109), the stay in Ciudad Real (1109), allusions to the older brother Juan (1071), and a civil engineer as a father (1070). That the character had, in a sense, nearly taken over his author can be ascertained from the many times that Miró actually signed himself as Sigüenza in letters and cards to his friends.[15] Concerning his character's nature, Miró was equally defensive as was made obvious when Benjamín Jarnés defined Sigüenza by saying, "He is an intelligence placed between the world and the reader," and Miró corrected him with the words, "No, he is a sensitivity."[16]

In the summer of 1902 Miró made two month-long trips to the leper colonies of Parcent. Two years later in *Del vivir,* Miró's "first personal book," as the poet Jorge Guillén (1893–1984) called it,[17] dealing—ironically—with the dying, Sigüenza makes a similar pilgrimage. In it Miró, however, does not tell of the death of these poor wretches but rather of their life sentence of privations and suffering, to whom every right, justice, or love is forbidden. Writing in the third person, the omniscient narrator fixes upon Sigüenza as his vantage point. Thus the reader knows not only what the protagonist feels and thinks, but also learns through Sigüenza's eyes all about the other characters' thoughts and feelings. The ten chapters, uniformly short, incorporate brief vignettes that take place along Sigüenza's route. Since *Del vivir* lacks much in the way of a plot, the itinerant adventures of Sigüenza constitute the sole structure and argument of the work. The character travels to Parcent and finds all of the expected miseries of the lepers but no compassion or charity on the part of their fellowmen. Cruelty, suffering, death, and a lack of fraternal sentiments are all Sigüenza encounters in the colony. These constitute the pervading themes of the work. Yet *Del vivir* manages to conclude on a hopeful if sad note. There are still some men, represented here especially by the doctor Don Ramón, capable of compassion, infinite patience, and altruism who can make the lepers' lives a little more bearable.

Libro de Sigüenza went through two editions in Miró's lifetime, the first in 1917 and the second in 1927. The definitive edition, issued in 1936, has three more chapters than the original version. The changes, resulting in the work's division into five parts and a total of thirty-three chapters, lend a more harmonious structure to *Libro de Sigüenza* and a cohesiveness to the myriad themes and focuses involved.[18]

Libro de Sigüenza may be Miró's most personal work, where life and art coincide in a perfect symbiosis. Into it the author pours his innermost thoughts—ranging throughout his thirty-eight years from the days as a boy in a Jesuit school up to the difficult times undergone while trying to secure a livelihood as a judge. Taking as a starting point a real occurrence, frequently autobiographical, Miró elevates it into a universal worth, transforming it artistically. Thus, the reader should not be surprised at the disparity of the narrative and the variety of vignettes included in this work whose only nexus appears to be the character Sigüenza appearing on every page.

In titling it *Libro* (book) Miró doubtless was suspect of its claims as a novel strictly speaking. Indeed, the novel label would be inexact for such an eclectic work, written piecemeal from 1903 until 1919, whose fragments appeared in several newspapers and magazines and whose individual chapters are, in turn, essays, parables, meditations, fables, memoirs, tales, and digressions of every sort. The title, *Libro de Sigüenza,* is a felicitous finding because of its exactness. The daily events in Sigüenza's life give it structural form. At times the happenings take on a certain autonomy from the rest; however, all are endowed with the same intense expression of individual will. Overall, the most discernible unifying element tying the chapters together is Sigüenza's vacillating, ingenuous, and hyperaesthetic spirit.

The themes of *Libro de Sigüenza* embrace a whole psychological gamut befitting a sensitive and impressionable spirit, responsive to primitive, natural, exquisite, and evil stimuli. Outstanding among such manifold themes are a nostalgia for the past (*ubi sunt?*, i.e.,

"Where have they gone?"); the love of nature (*locus amoemus,* i.e.,
"pleasant surroundings"); *beatus ille,* (i.e., "blessed are those who
choose the country . . ."); the alienation of man (see in Unamuno's
chapter the section on existentialism), and man as a wanderer through
life *(homo viator).* Other topics such as progress viewed with skepticism, the devotion for the Holy Scriptures, xenophobia and mis-
anthropy (fear of strangers and loathing of one's fellowmen
respectively), though not as fully developed, complete the thematic
scheme of *Libro de Sigüenza,* qualifying it as not only Miró's most
personal work, but also his most direct and diverse. The words of
its concluding paragraph, "Mirad las aves del cielo . . ." ("consider
the birds of the air . . .") confer upon *Libro de Sigüenza* a closed
circular structure, given that it begins with the same words of St.
Luke (12:24), while suggesting a hopeful Christian circle of eternal
renewal not unlike that of *Del vivir.*

Años y leguas is the last of his books that Miró saw published.
The year was 1928. He began writing it in the summer months of
1922 during his stay in Polop de la Marina (Alicante) on the Mediterranean coast. The title *Años y leguas,* measures of time and space, is
an unadorned image not only of this work, where the landscape and
the passing of time structurally buttress the content, but also of
Del vivir and *Libro de Sigüenza* because it sums up symbolically
Sigüenza's entire existence and marks its end. The years and the
leagues are the vital coordinates that guide the life of the hero along
Miró's pages from 1904 until 1928. *Años y leguas* turns out to be
a suitable conclusion for the earlier books whose trajectory ends
here.

The arranged structure by sections is such that, as the narrative
unfolds, the chapters acquire more and more subdivisions—one for
the first chapter, five for the seventeenth and last. As the work
progresses the pace of the narration slows; there is an almost absolute
lack of dates; time passes all but unnoticeably in a hazy, slow-
moving continuity. No new places appear in *Años y leguas;* Sigüenza
passes through where he has been before; this is a journey of return,
but the impressions differ from those of twenty years earlier gathered
in *Del vivir.* Everything has become less concrete; Miró is less willing
to be precise. As Sigüenza grows old, he withdraws increasingly
into himself. In *Del vivir* he had felt a tender compassion for the
lepers of Parcent, in *Libro de Sigüenza* he had walked about the streets
of the city surrounded by people but alienated from them, and now

in *Años y leguas,* outside of the urban chaos, he seeks the solitude of the countryside in a renewed emphasis of the *beatus ille* theme. The other themes are equally familiar: death and time (*memento mori,* i.e., "remember death," and *tempus fugit,* i.e., "fleeting time"), cruelty viewed with some irony, and above all the beauty and timelessness of nature viewed in the Alicante landscapes.

Años y leguas is a book that quickly satiates its reader. The morose, dense, slow narrative tempo is a contributing factor. Scenes follow each other in slow motion, descriptions possess a heavy pictorial quality similar to those canvases done with a palette knife instead of a brush, and dialogues—one way to accelerate the narrative tempo—are nonexistent (Sigüenza walks alone most of the time) and instead, long paragraphs of scenic proportions multiply. Miró's jeweler's eye and his lush style lend themselves to this rich prose full of an archaic, recondite, and poetic vocabulary. Of course, it also elicited on occasion censorious comments such as the one by Ortega cited earlier. However, the *tempo lento* that so characterizes *Años y leguas* comes mostly from within the work itself and its ultimate significance. Fundamentally, it is a more tranquil work, more contemplative than *Del vivir* or *Libro de Sigüenza,* because it reaches the longed-for-peace at the end of a life's journey. As the protagonist begins to look back, most of his life behind him, more meditation results. It remains only for Sigüenza to find some significance in all of his wanderings and, with the perspective so acquired, to make amends for whatever missteps may have been taken. Once that is done, as he confronts the massive Rock of Ifach, aware of his own mortality in the face of a permanent nature, the narrative is extinguished as dawn breaks, and Miró serenely bids good-bye to his alter ego Sigüenza and humbly takes leave of his reader.

The Oleza Novels

Following the publication of the short novelette *El abuelo del rey* (The grandfather of the king) in 1915, Miró reconstructed his earlier story of 1909, *Los amores de Antón Hernando,* expanded it to novelistic proportions, and with the new title *Niño y grande,* published it in 1922. This work is a love story of decadentist overtones whose aristocratic protagonist, consumed by self-doubt, reveals Miró's adeptness at psychological character portrayal. Probably written as early as 1912,[19] *El abuelo del rey,* though brief, manages to relate the saga of three generations of the prominent Fernández Pons family in the eastern Spanish city of Serosca, the frustrated lives of the three men heading each generation, and the changes experienced in an urban society at the end of the nineteenth century.

This theme of how progress changes the traditional status quo of an established provincial town is perhaps the main theme from which all others derive in this, Miró's most ambitious and successful novelistic undertaking: the bipartite work *Our Father San Daniel* and its continuation, *El obispo leproso*. Though published separately in 1921 and 1926, respectively, the novels' common themes, shared characters, and their singular location in the fictional town of Oleza (modeled after Orihuela, in the province of Alicante) leave no doubt that they are one fictional microcosm. In addition, both volumes are subtitled "Novela de capellanes y devotos" (A novel of priests and worshippers). The internal chronology of the work separates the two halves by eight years, the story unfolding between spring of 1880 and summer of 1897. The theme of progress as a disquieting factor which slowly unleashes and reveals all of the characters' pent-up feelings and passions is depicted in the coming of a railroad that will open up Oleza's repressed society to the outside world—the capital city of Murcia. The foreshadowed struggle between the secular or liberal branch of this society and the clerically dominated segment materializes and continues throughout both parts of the work, lending it a strong narrative skeleton—a novelistic quality for whose absence Miró had previously been criticized.

In *Our Father San Daniel,* the patriarch Don Daniel Egea and his daughter Paulina, happy and well-meaning landowners, are tormented by the sinister figure of the fanatical Don Alvaro Galindo who marries Paulina and separates father and daughter forever. The birth of a son, Pablo, signals the end of this first part and the beginning of the *El obispo leproso.* Here the plot focuses on the lives of this family, which also includes Alvaro's domineering sister Elvira, and the son's rearing, ending with his adulterous relationship with an older woman when he becomes seventeen.

If these plots seem uncomplicated, it is because Miró emphasizes more the characters, their lives and relationships and the city's milieu than action per se. Around them the author builds numerous episodes which, though arguably autonomous, are woven into the fabric of the main theme and form part of the whole tapestry that constitutes the novel *Our Father San Daniel–El obispo leproso.* The duality of the work begins with the physical division of Oleza's urban setting by a river that bisects it. This first typographical separation pits one social class against another. Within them, further subdivision according to political and religious adherences ensues. On the one hand, the ultraconservative Carlists, defenders of tradition and religion, face the liberal party made up of reformists and more progressive types. On the other hand, the religious community is itself split, each side backing the corresponding political faction. The Jesuits, whose college in Orihuela Miró attended in his youth, lend support to the Carlists locally and to their cause nationally—the 1870s Carlist War begins with the novel—while the benevolent bishop views with some satisfaction the projects embraced by the liberals.

Above all else the reader perceives the oppressiveness engendered by theocratic rule in a town where the ringing of the cathedral's carillon dictates the comings and goings of its citizenry. Just as often, passions, emotions, and feelings are not repressed as a result of religious mandate; they are quashed by the austere obsessions of secular individuals. The store of Don Alvaro and his family symbolizes what Miró most loathed about the church: its all-too-rigid control of Spanish society at the turn of the century. The easygoing Paulina is made to live a cloistered life of penance, self-denial, and religious ritual by her husband and her embittered sister-in-law, the prudish spinster Elvira. Even the mother-son relationship between Paulina and Pablo becomes an object of Don Alvaro's prohibitions, so that tears and stolen caresses are all of the affections extant though forbidden. In the end these pent-up passions become so great that they engender excesses in their life-asserting manifestations. The sadistic Elvira, sexually crazed, attempts the rape of her nephew. Pablo, frustrated through most of his teenage years, falls in love and commits adultery with the young María Fulgencia, married to a man thirty years her senior. Even during Holy Week the church cannot prevent the overtly sensual aspects of religious liturgy that in Oleza happen to coincide with the fragrant flowering of orange and lemon blossoms. Young people and old alike become intoxicated with the celebrations that allow for open, crowded meetings where the smells of the blossoms mix with those of incense. The colors of the flowers and the pageantry further excite the senses as everyone sings and touches one another.

The church itself is looked at critically, though not with such uniform severity as Ayala had used, through its institutions (the Episcopal see, the Jesuit College), its practices (the paganism and rituals of Holy Week and Corpus Christi), and its representatives. From the benevolent and long-suffering leper bishop—never a central figure, though a constantly felt presence—and the simple Franciscan priest Don Magín—much like Miró himself as it has been suggested[20]—to the hateful Padre Bellod who delights in the slow roasting of the poor church mice for having "profaned" the basilica, Miró offers up a complete tableau of ecclesiastic provincialism both at its best and at its worst.

Our Father San Daniel and *El obispo leproso* are difficult novels to read. Narrative interest, as always in this Generation of 1914, lags. The characters and their interrelationships have become more important than the telling of a story. To this it must be added that Miró's complex, lushly descriptive, and sometimes arcane style forces the reader to pause often and think. It is inconceivable that either of these works or any of Miró's other fiction could be read at one sitting. It is too rich to be quickly enjoyed or digested. Moreover, Miró's prose fiction, and especially the Oleza novels, need the participation of the reader for a full understanding.

Addressing himself to his art as a novelist, Miró once declared: "Creo que en *El obispo leproso* se afirma más mi concepto sobre la novela: decir las cosas por insinuación. No es menester—estéticamente—agotar los episodios" (I believe that in *The Leper Bishop* my concept of the novel is further affirmed: to tell by insinuating. It isn't necessary—aesthetically [speaking]—to overdo each episode).[21] No one who has read Gabriel Miró's fiction can challenge the beauty of his prose, the newness of his novelistic concept, or his deep humanism. After all, his literature completes a full circle from the 1904 *Del vivir* to the 1926 *El obispo leproso,* wherein his concern for the most ostracized segment of mankind—those plagued by the biblical scourge of leprosy—is patent.

Chapter Seven
Conclusion: Minor Novelists of the Period 1898 to 1936

All of the members of the Generation of 1898, except the poet Antonio Machado,[1] wrote novels, yet not every one of them deserves to be called a novelist in the truest sense of the term. Only Unamuno, Valle, and, above all, Baroja merit the label unequivocally. Of those remaining, Ramiro de Maeztu wrote just one novel, *La guerra del Transvaal y los misterios de la Banca de Londres* (The Transvaal war and the mysteries of London's banks). It appeared in serialized installments, from 1 April, 1900 to 6 January, 1901 in the newspaper *El País*. Published for the first time in book form as recently as 1974 (forty-four years after its author's death), this novel is a six-hundred page account of political, financial, and sociological plotting in London, Johannesburg, Kimberly, and other distant places at the time of the war in South Africa. There are diamonds, gold, intrigue, and love besides, all with an eye to appealing to the widest possible reading public of the Madrid daily. That Maeztu was neither too sure nor too proud of the novel's literary worth is confirmed by the pseudonym artfully fabricated in the pages of *El País* prior to the appearance of the work itself. Van Poel Krupp, a Dutch newspaper correspondent and adventurer with firsthand knowledge of the Transvaal conflict, serves as the mask behind which Maeztu perpetrated this literary hoax.[2]

Valle himself was not above similar undertakings, done strictly for economic reasons. His novel *La cara de Dios* (The face of God), written in 1900, was commissioned by the publishing house "Editorial de J. García," for which he received the then unheard-of sum of 1,150 pesetas. It amounts to little more than a narrative version of Carlos Arniches's (1866–1943) play of the same title. As it turns out, Valle stretched the serialized work to over five hundred pages so that he could collect additional revenues, a feat that forced him not only to plagiarize Arniches's drama, for which he had received permission from the author himself, but to invent new segments and even, according to Julio Andrade, to copy word for word several chapters from Dostoevski's *Nietochka Nezwanova*.[3] Seventy-four years after its appearance in serialized form it was finally published as a volume.[4]

Azorín's Near-Novels

José Martínez Ruiz, "Azorín," wrote sixteen novels, yet his worth as a novelist has been forever in dispute. For the most part Spanish critics, among them José Ortega y Gasset,[5] Luis Granjel,[6] and Eugenio G. de Nora,[7] have cast grave doubts on his novelistic aptitude. On the other hand, such American scholars as E. Inman Fox,[8] Kathleen M. Glenn,[9] Leon Livingstone,[10] and Robert E. Lott[11] have praised Azorín's novels as vanguardist examples of the genre. This nearly uniform split between Spanish and American criticism lies at the very heart of what constitutes a novelistic archetype. The former group succumbs to defining the novel within the traditional canons of an extended narrative with attendant subplots and characters that either develop (i.e., change) or reveal themselves as the story unfolds in a chronological or internal sequential order. Few, if any, of Azorín's novels fulfill such a concept. The latter critics allow a broader, less rigid definition of the genre, so that the terms surrealist novel, antinovel, novel-within-a-novel, amorphous novel, and other similar labels are used at one time or another by Fox, Glenn, Livingstone, and Lott.

The first of nine children, José Martínez Ruiz was born on 8 June, 1873 in Monóvar (Alicante) where his father was mayor of the city. The son of wealthy landowners, the lawyer Isidro Martínez and María Luisa Ruiz, José attended a private Catholic school run by Piarist monks in Yecla before enrolling as a law student at the University of Valencia. After eight years of largely fruitless studies, he left for Madrid in 1896 without receiving a degree. Unanamo, Baroja, Maeztu, and Valle converged on the Spanish capital around the same time. Like them and perhaps because of them, Azorín went through an extreme liberal phase that verged on anarchism. It showed in his politics and in his newspaper articles of the times.[12] Yet gradually his archconservative upbringing reclaimed its hold on José, and he, almost before any of his colleagues, turned from rebel to moderate and eventually to right-winger. In 1905 he joined the staff of the influential *El Imparcial* and the monarchist *ABC* (an affiliation that lasted until his death in 1967) dailies; between 1907 and 1919 he was elected to the *Cortes* (Parliament) seven times; from 1917 to 1918 he served as undersecretary of education; and in 1924 he was elected to the august Spanish Royal Academy of Letters. In 1908, at the age of thirty-five, he married Julia Guinda Urzangui, and the couple—childless—lived an uneventful existence on Zorrilla Street in Madrid, interrupted only by the three years (1936–39) of the Civil War spent in Paris, and by his travels—most of them on foot or by horse-drawn carriage—throughout Spain. Azorín wrote tirelessly until shortly before his death at the age of ninety-four so that his works number over one hundred titles, most of them collections of essays, though he also wrote ten plays[13]—largely without success—as well as literary biographies, travelogues, and the sixteen novels mentioned above.

His most notable are the Antonio Azorín trilogy *La voluntad* (Will), *Antonio Azorín,* and *Las confesiones de un pequeño filósofo* (The confessions of a little philosopher) published in succession in 1902, 1903, and 1904. These make up a single opus, autobiographical in nature, dealing with the development of a character and a literary personality that was to take over the author's own as José Martínez Ruiz assumed his protagonist's name Azorín ("little goshawk") with which he signed all of his work after 1904. The three are reflective volumes where a lack of resolve turns the young hero into a resigned and melancholy intellectual, incapable of any but the most contemplative pursuits.

After an eighteen-year hiatus Azorín wrote a cycle of two novels based on the classic love theme of Don Juan Tenorio: *Don Juan* (1922) and *Doña Inés* (1925). Neither, however, follows the traditional story line. *Don Juan,* in fact, portrays a repentant seducer who, now old, after a serious illness wishes to atone for his sins and devotes the rest of his life to humanitarian deeds. Don Juan del Prado y Ramos ends up as Brother Juan in a curious parallel to Unamuno's 1934 play *El hermano Juan* (Brother Juan) where women seduce their victim Juan. *Doña Inés,* generally viewed as Azorín's finest novelistic effort, focuses on Inés de Silva, a rich and beautiful woman, as she begins to lose her youth. And yet, although one senses the story is there, Azorín fails to fully develop it. Instead, much like *Don Juan, Doña Inés* turns out to be a fragmented series of vignettes with too much left unsaid to satisfy the reader. Only three occurrences take place in the novel: Doña Inés receives a letter of rejection from her lover (largely surmised), she is kissed by a young man in the cathedral of Segovia (a short three-sentence moment), and she moves to Argentina where she founds an orphanage. Nothing else happens, and the rest is a slow consideration of Azorín's favorite themes: the passing of time, the difficulties of writing a book, and the interior duplication which make most lives seem to pass through moments of déjà vu.

A third stage in Azorín's novelistic career follows, which he called *Nuevas obras* (New works) and most critics deem his surrealist period, that brought forth *Félix Vargas* in 1928 (later retitled *El caballero inactual* [The timeless gentleman]), *Superrealismo* in 1929 (later retitled *El libro de Levante* [The book of Levant]), and *Pueblo* (The people) in 1930. These are experimental novels largely lacking in plot, inundated with minute descriptions and free associations of ideas, and dwelling on the varying psychological states of the characters. The last two amount to no more than drafts for possible novels, so incomplete and unsatisfying is the sum of their pages.

The final and most fecund period of Azorín as a novelist lasted but two years in the early forties when *El escritor* (The writer), *Capricho* (Capriccio), *El enfermo* (The sick man), *María Fontán, Salvadora de Olbena*, and *La isla sin aurora* (The island without dawn) appeared from 1942 to 1944. The first three offer familiar preoccupations to the reader of Azorín: the writer and his work, the writer and his life, the work and its myriad possibilities. *Salvadora de Olbena*, doubtless the best of the series, recalls the frustrated love story earlier seen in *Doña Inés*. Subtitled "Novela romántica," its themes are, once again, lost beauty (a young rich widow about to lose her looks), the passing of time (a fixation with clocks), and the anxieties that life's choices bring. As in *Doña Inés*, nothing is allowed to happen; Azorín does not permit the novel to develop. *La isla sin aurora* is a piece of escapist fiction, an aesthetic allegory[14] totally removed from reality and filled with oneiric and mythological symbolism that clearly marks the conclusion of a trajectory. Arriving at this dead end, however, did not compel Azorín to try a new approach. It proved to be his last novel.

An admirable prose writer, Azorín seems incapable of spinning a yarn. He is no storyteller, one of the key requisites for any serious novelist. If Azorín disappoints as a novelist in the end it is because his fiction merely portrays characters instead of allowing them to live. The feeble, almost nonexistent plots frustrate the reader who despairs at the sameness of themes, the drawn-out descriptions of minutiae, the lack of memorable characters, the constant identification of protagonist-narrator-author, the fragmentary nature of the tenuous narrative, and the slow tempo of the story. Azorín's novel cannot satisfy because its fictional microcosm is too small, too incomplete, and too sterile, seemingly erected on the base of a cultivated, artificial prose style the contents of which do not withstand translation. Ortega may have never made a more perceptive literary comment than when he labeled Azorín's art "Primores de lo vulgar" (Elegances of the commonplace).[15]

Nothing New

There are several novelists who began writing in the early 1900s, while the authors of the Generation of 1898 dominated the literary scene, and who continued publishing until most of those belonging to the Generation of 1914 had vanished from view. These writers belonged to neither of the two generations nor did they constitute a group of their own. Instead they created individually, independent of any school or affiliation. All of them enjoyed a wide reading public, a mass audience that appreciated the traditional nature of their works, their indisputable adeptness as gifted storytellers and their prolific output. Among the most admired of these popular novelists who wrote from 1910 up to the 1950s, Ricardo León (1877–1943), Concha Espina (1877–1955), and Wenceslao Fernández Flórez (1885–1964) merit the most note.

Ricardo León, while repeatedly lambasted by most critics,[16] reached a wider audience than any other novelist of his time. His novels depict in a convoluted manner an anachronistic and highly idealized Spain where patriotic, Christian, and heroic protagonists triumph over every conceivable evil, no matter how lacking in verisimilitude. Of León's seventeen long novels, his 1908 *Casta de hidalgos* (Breed of scions), the 1910 *Amor de los amores* (Foremost love), and the 1943 *Cristo en los infiernos* (Christ in hell) are best remembered. That León's kind of literature appealed not only to the average reader but to some more influential ones cannot be denied in view of his election to the Spanish Royal Academy in 1912 at the extraordinarily young age of thirty-five.

Concha Espina, a sometime poet as is evident in the lyrical well-turned passages of her prose fiction, also produced seventeen extensive novels among her fifty-odd works. Writing even while blind in her later years, Espina produced interesting narratives, easily described as sentimental realism. *La niña de Luzmela* (The girl from Luzmela, 1909), *La esfinge maragata* (The Leonese Sphinx, 1913), *El metal de los muertos* (Dead men's metal), 1920), and *Altar mayor* (The main altar, 1926) are Concha Espina's most representative works. Hers, unlike Ricardo León's, have a place not only in the best-seller lists of that time but also in any history of Spanish literature.

The youngest writer of this type is the Galician Wenceslao Fernández Flórez, arguably the best of the lot. A conservative (some would say a reactionary, based on his friendship with his countryman, the dictator Franco) and a successful journalist all his life (a political columnist for Madrid's *ABC* for over half a century), Fernández Flórez wrote nearly thirty novels, which merit closer attention than most scholars have been willing to admit.[17] He managed not only to mesmerize his readers (fourteen thousand copies of his novel *Los que no fuimos a la guerra* [Those of us who didn't go to war] were sold within a two-week period in 1930)[18] and to secure a handsome living from his writings and the adaptations of his novels into films (more books by Fernández Flórez were made into movies than any other Spanish novelist up to that time including Galdós and Blasco),[19] but also to convince the critics and the literary establishment of the worth of his fiction—as his award, among many received throughout his life, of the Premio Nacional de Literatura in 1926 (shared jointly with Pérez de Ayala and Concha Espina) for the novel *El secreto de Barba Azul* (Bluebeard's secret) and his election to the Spanish Royal Academy in 1935 can attest. His novels are steeped in a lyrical melancholy and often humorous realism that some[20] have called typically Galician, thinking back perhaps to the misty and nostalgic verse of that region's most famous poet, Rosalía de Castro (1837–85). *Volvoreta* (Butterfly, 1917), *La casa de la lluvia* (The rain house, 1925), and *El bosque animado* (The living forest, 1944) constitute a rare literary phenomenon in the sense that their popularity in no way detracts from their high literary worth. Several others among Fernández Flórez's many novels are equally deserving.

Today, in the last quarter of the twentieth century, these three novelists have been largely forgotten in spite of their former popularity. True, their contribution to the development of the novel is almost nil, but the influence of Ricardo León, Concha Espina, and Wenceslao Fernández Flórez on the tastes of a reading public as limited as Spain had in the early 1900s (in 1915 sixty percent of Spain's twenty-three million inhabitants could not read or write)[21] was so disproportionately large that they must not be ignored.

Innovators

After Ramón Pérez de Ayala and Gabriel Miró, Benjamín Jarnés (1888–1943) is the most important novelist of their Generation of 1914, though his significance falls well below theirs. He was an assiduous writer who felt most at home in the purist circle of authors whose high priest was the philosopher José Ortega y Gasset. Ortega's pulpit and the outlet for his disciples' writings was the newly founded (1923) journal with the pretentious title of *Revista de Occidente* (Journal of the western world). It eventually became the symbol of a small publishing empire still flourishing today. In the pages of the *Revista de Occidente* Jarnés published some of his best essays and, through the newly created "Editorial Revista de Occidente," the inaugural edition of his first novel *El profesor inútil* (The useless professor).

A student for the priesthood at the San Carlos Seminary and later at the Pontifical University of Zaragoza, Jarnés gave up the idea of a religious vocation when drafted into the army in 1910. After his tour of duty he considered a teaching career and enrolled at the Zaragoza Normal School, but he eventually joined the army reserve corps where he rose to the rank of captain. Jarnés married Gregoria Bergua and the couple moved permanently to Madrid in 1920. At that time his first articles began appearing (though three years earlier he had contributed several pieces to the Catholic magazine *El Pilar*) with some regularity, and he fell under Ortega's spell. *El profesor inútil* (1926), Jarnés's first and one of his three best novels, puts into fiction the message that Ortega had begun proclaiming in the 1925 treatise *La deshumanización del arte e ideas sobre la novela* (*The Dehumanization of Art and Thoughts on the Novel*). Jarnés two other small masterpieces, *Paula y Paulita* and *Locura y muerte de nadie* (The madness and death of nobody), out of a total of eleven full-length novels, both were published in 1929 and signal the end of his greatest creative period, even though his last narrative work of fiction published under the pseudonym of Julio Aznar did not appear until twenty years later. Typical Jarnés novels belabor the lives of ordinary characters whose problems pale by comparison with reality. Written in a lyrical style but with a detachment worthy of the Orteguian "dehumanization," Jarnés novels do not move the reader. They have not aged well either, a fact recognized with pained honesty by Jarnés himself one year before his death. He wrote then, "The time is past when a writer could allow himself the luxury of dazzling with lights, reflections, shadows, obscurities. . . . That is to say, with the luxury of his own ambiguities. The public ends up liking only a sane writer."[22]

Similarly inclined novelists of the period were Antonio Espina (1894–), Mauricio Bacarisse (1895–1931), and Claudio de la Torre (1897–). The first of these, like Jarnés, collaborated in the *Revista de Occidente,* and the others received the prestigious Premio Nacional de Literatura for at least one of their novels. They, together with Benjamín Jarnés, brought a breath of fresh air into Spanish fiction during the twenties and thirties insofar as they were among the very few who read and introduced to Spain (and sometimes translated) major European novelists such as Aldous Huxley (1894–1963), James Joyce (1882–1941), Franz Kafka (1883–1924), and Marcel Proust (1871–1922). Their desire to innovate led them to produce original but not very creative novels that though indifferently received by the public were lauded by the critics. These fictional experiments, unpopular at the time of their publication, cannot claim today even the attention of scholars themselves. Like Jarnés's novels, theirs have also aged noticeably and much too quickly to be taken into account as anything but vanguardist experimental literature.

Looking Back

In a long look back surveying the generations to which these sixteen writers belong, two stand out above the rest when judged from a strictly novelistic vantage point. The purest novelist in the traditional sense is Baroja; in the modern sense, it is Pérez de Ayala. The former entertains the reader and amuses himself. Baroja's audience can afford to relax and get comfortable with his novels; Ayala's must prepare itself to work in order to derive any enjoyment. While Baroja simply perfected the art of storytelling—no small feat in itself—in the novel, Ayala expanded the boundaries of novelistic format in a lasting way. The perspectivism of multiple points of view in *Belarmino y Apolonio,* to cite one of the most obvious examples of Ayala's innovative narrative craft, helps to make such avant garde works as Camilo José Cela's (1916–) *La colmena (The Beehive)* in 1951 or even Julio Cortázar's (1914–84) *Rayuela (Hopscotch)* in 1963 conceivable at all. In a sense, then, Baroja's appeal was immediate and greater, but I suspect that Ayala's, though always smaller, will remain constant and endure as long as Baroja's—perhaps longer. Seldom does one feel compelled to reread the older novelist, for he mostly has a story to tell, whereas Ayala's works rarely reveal themselves in one or even two readings. There is always a need to go back to uncover still more.

Following, if not the death, the decline of these two masters came a period of novelistic sterility, after the 1930s, despite the youngest authors considered above whom I labeled "innovators" (Jarnés, Espina, Bacarisse, de la Torre, de la Ossa), that lasted until such postwar figures as Cela with his *La familia de Pascual Duarte (The Family of Pascual Duarte)* in 1942 and Carmen Laforet (1921–) with her *Nada* (Nothing) in 1944 surprised the reading public, shook their fellow authors out of their lethargy, and encouraged the renaissance of the contemporary Spanish novel into its second half century.

Notes and References

Chapter One

1. From approximately 1876 to 1882 there are over one hundred and thirty references to naturalism in the Spanish press. See Gifford Davis, "The Critical Reception of Naturalism in Spain before *La cuestión palpitante*," *Hispanic Review* 22 (1954):97.

2. F. W. J. Hemmings, ed., *The Age of Realism* (Middlesex: Penguin Books, 1974), 285.

3. Galdós's *La desheredada* (1881) is generally acknowledged as the first naturalist novel written in Spanish. His *El amigo Manso* (1882) and *El Doctor Centeno* (1883) exhibit similar traits.

4. Eduardo Betoret-Paris, *El costumbrismo regional en la obra de Blasco Ibáñez* (Valencia: Fomento Cultural de Ediciones, 1958), 317.

5. Ibid., 33.

6. In a letter to the critic Julio Cejador y Frauca partially reproduced in the introduction to Blasco's *Obras completas,* vol. 1 (Madrid: Aguilar, 1958), 17.

7. Ibid., 15.

8. Betoret-Paris, *El costumbrismo,* 39–40.

9. A. Grove Day and Edgar C. Knowlton, Jr., *V. Blasco Ibáñez* (New York, 1972), 61.

10. Prologue to *La barraca* (New York: Las Américas, n.d.), 8.

11. Day and Knowlton, *Blasco Ibáñez,* 64.

12. José Ortega y Gasset, *Meditaciones del Quijote: Ideas sobre la novela* (Madrid: Espasa-Calpe, 1964), 203.

13. Cited by Emiliano Díez-Echarri and J. M. Roca Franquesa, *Historia de la literatura española e hispanoamericana* (Madrid: Aguilar, 1960), 1118.

Chapter Two

1. Luis S. Granjel, *La generación literaria del 98* (Salamanca, 1971), 164.

2. Vicente Marrero, *Maeztu* (Madrid: Rialp, 1955), 159.

3. Ricardo Landeira, *Ramiro de Maeztu* (Boston: Twayne Publishers, 1978), 22–26.

4. Cited by Marrero, *Maeztu,* 720.

5. Julián Marías, *Miguel de Unamuno* (Madrid, 1950). See especially chap. 3, "La novela personal," 42–66.

6. Emilio Salcedo, *Vida de Don Miguel* (Salamanca, 1964), 38.

7. Ibid., 338.

8. Germán Bleiberg, Julián Marías et al., eds. *Diccionario de literatura española* (Madrid: Revista de Occidente, 1972), 900. See also the article exploring this notion by Ricardo Gullón, "La novela personal de don Miguel de Unamuno," *La Torre* 35–36 (July–December 1961):93–115.

9. (*Del sentimiento trágico de la vida en los hombres y en los pueblos* (Madrid: Editorial Plenitud, 1965). In chapter 2, "El punto de partida," Unamuno writes: "¿Por qué quiero saber de dónde vengo y a dónde voy, de dónde viene y a dónde va lo que me rodea, y qué significa todo esto? Porque no quiero morirme del todo, y quiero saber si he de morirme o no definitivamente. Y si no muero, ¿qué será de mí?; y si muero, ya nada tiene sentido. Y hay tres soluciones: a) o sé que me muero del todo, y entonces la desesperación irremediable, o b) sé que no muero del todo, y entonces la resignación, o c) no puedo saber ni una ni otra cosa, y entonces la resignación en la desesperación, o ésta en aquélla, una resignación desesperada, o una desesperación resignada, y la lucha" (30–31).

10. Gullón, "La novela personal," 93.

11. Unamuno is rumored to have worked on another novel prior to and at the same time as *Paz en la guerra*. The project went through four title changes: *Nuevo mundo, El reino del hombre, Eugenio Rodero,* and *El reino de Dios*. See Salcedo, *Vida,* 421, and Armando Zubizarreta, *Tras las huellas de Unamuno* (Madrid, 1960), 47–109.

12. *San Manuel Bueno, mártir y tres historias más* (Madrid: Espasa-Calpe, 1942), 29.

13. Ibid., 59.

14. Pelayo H. Hernández, "Más sobre 'San Manuel Bueno, mártir' de Unamuno," *Revista Hispanica Moderna* 29 (1963):261.

15. *Recuerdos de niñez y mocedad* (Madrid: Espasa-Calpe, 1942), 9.

16. *Abel Sánchez* (Madrid: Espasa-Calpe, 1940), 11.

17. Ibid., 13.

18. For a general treatise on "La belle dame sans merci," see chapter 2 of Mario Praz's invaluable *The Romantic Agony* (London: Oxford University Press, 1970), 197–300. For a closer look at Unamuno's treatment of the type see David W. Foster's "The 'Belle dame sans merci' in the Fiction of Miguel de Unamuno," *Symposium,* Winter 1966, pp. 321–28. Foster, though he looks at *Niebla, La tía Tula, Dos madres,* and *El Marqués de Lumbría,* inexplicably omits *Abel Sánchez*.

19. *Cómo se hace una novela* (Madrid: Alianza Editorial, 1966), 122. Here Unamuno wrote: "Héteme aquí ante estas páginas blancas, mi porvenir, tratando de derramar mi vida a fin de continuar viviendo, de darme la vida, de arrancarme a la muerte de cada instante."

20. Jean Cassou not only translated it but also wrote a "Portrait d'Unamuno" for "Comment on fait un roman." Both appeared together in *Mercure de France,* 15 May, 1926.

21. Gullón, "La novela personal," 93–115.

Chapter Three

1. Beatrice P. Patt, *Pío Baroja* (New York, 1971), 196–98.

2. Ibid.

3. Ernest Hemingway is quoted as saying to Baroja: "Allow me to pay this small tribute to you who taught so much to those of us who wanted to be writers when we were young. I deplore the fact that you have not yet received a Nobel Prize, especially when it was given to so many who deserved it less, like me, who am only an adventurer." Among the gifts Hemingway bore to Baroja was a copy of his *Farewell to Arms* with the dedication "in homage from his disciple" (*Time,* 29 October 1956, p. 47).

4. *Memorias,* vol. 1 (Madrid: Minotauro, 1955), 131.

5. Some of the articles and short stories written then are closely linked to these biographical experiences. See Ricardo L. Landeira and Janet W. Díaz's "Irony and Death in Pío Baroja's 'Los panaderos,' " in *Studies in Honor of Gerald E. Wade,* ed. Sylvia Bowman et al. (Madrid: Editorial Porrúa, 1979), 121–32.

6. D. L. Shaw, ed., *Pío Baroja, El mundo es ansí* (Oxford: Pergamon Press, 1970), 5.

7. *Obras completas,* 8 vols. (Madrid, 1946–51), 7:807–915.

8. Ibid.

9. Pedro Salinas, "Don Pío Baroja y el romance 'plebeyo'," in his *Ensayos de literatura hispánica* (Madrid: Aguilar, 1967), 355. Salinas refers to him as "el amargado y amargante don Pío Baroja; poco había perdonado el señor Baroja en este mundo, y sus obras en prosa acumulan vituperios y desprecio para casi todo lo humano y lo divino."

10. Shaw, ed., *Pío Baroja,* 14.

11. Eugenio G. de Nora, *La novela española contemporánea (1898–1927),* 3 vols. (Madrid, 1963), 3:134.

12. The French novelist Honoré de Balzac (1799–1850) is the first credited with using the same character in several works.

13. Emilio González López, *El arte narrativo de Pío Baroja: Las trilogías* (New York: Las Américas, 1971), 145.

14. *La busca* (Barcelona: Editorial Planeta, 1968), 295: " '¡Estos ya no son buenos!' La frase le había producido una impresión profunda. ¿Por qué no era bueno él? ¿Por qué? Examinó su vida."

15. Nora, *La novela española,* 167.

16. E. Inman Fox, "Baroja and Schopenhauer: *El árbol de la ciencia*," *Revue de littérature comparée* 37 (1963):355.

17. Ibid., 353.

18. *El árbol de la ciencia* (Madrid: Alianza Editorial, 1972), 96. Dr. Iturrioz says to Andrés: "ante la vida no hay más que dos soluciones prácticas para el hombre sereno: o la abstención y la contemplación indiferente de todo, o la acción limitándose a un círculo pequeño."

19. "Hurtado era entusiasta de Espronceda" (*El árbol de la ciencia* [Madrid: Alianza Editorial, 1972], 11).

20. See Ricardo López Landeira, "La desilusión poética de Espronceda: Realidad y Poesía Irreconciliables," *Boletín de la Real Academia Española* 205 (May–August 1975):307–29.

21. "Este muchacho no tenía fuerza para vivir. . . . Pero había en él algo de precursor" (*El árbol de la ciencia* [Madrid: Alianza Editorial, 1972], 248).

22. Shaw, *Pío Baroja*, 16.

23. "Sí; todo es violencia, todo es crueldad en la vida. ¿Y qué hacer? No se puede abstenerse de vivir, no se puede parar, hay que seguir marchando hasta el final" (ibid., 183).

24. Samuel Beckett, *I Can't Go On, I'll Go On*, ed. Richard W. Seaver (New York: Grove Press, 1976), 331.

25. *El árbol de la ciencia*, 96.

Chapter Four

1. *Sonata de primavera y sonata de estío* (Madrid: Espasa-Calpe, 1963), 107.

2. On 23 June 1981, nearly half a century after his death, King Juan Carlos I established the "Marquesado de Bradomín" in Valle's memory and in his honor.

3. José Rubia Barcia, "A Synoptic View of Valle Inclán's Life and Works," in *Ramón del Valle-Inclán: An Appraisal of His Life and Works*, ed. Anthony N. Zahareas (New York, 1968), 4.

4. *Femeninas* contains the following stories: "La generala," "Tula Varona," "La niña Chole," "La Condesa de Cela," "Octavia Santino," and "Rosarito."

5. Ramón Gómez de la Serna reproduces the entire poem in his biography *Don Ramón María del Valle-Inclán* (Madrid: Espasa-Calpe, 1959), 28:

> Desde Toledo a Busdongo,
> desde la China al Japón.
> no hay nada como el jabón
> de los príncipes del Congo.

Retorciendo la filástica
un cordelero enfermó;
pero al punto se curó.
¿Cómo? Con la harina plástica.

En toda fiesta onomástica
yo os digo:—¡Comed, bebed!
¡Atracaos! ¡Absorbed
la dosis de harina plástica!

Meanwhile, Domingo García Sabell, in his introduction to Valle's *La cara de Dios* (Madrid: Taurus, 1972), 22, gives a shorter and different version:

¿La pesadilla fantástica
os agobia, en invernales
noches? ¡Los estomacales
jugos con la Harina Plástica
reconfortad, animales!

6. Rubia Barcia, "A Synoptic View," 11.
7. Quoted as "El signo de los intelectuales españoles es idéntico al de los gitanos: vivir perseguidos por la guardia civil" (Rubia Barcia, "A Synoptic View," 19–20).
8. Bleiberg et al., *Diccionario,* 253.
9. *Martes de carnaval* includes the following plays: *Las galas del difunto, Los cuernos de don Friolera,* and *La hija del capitán.*
10. In a prefatory note to the *Spring Sonata,* Valle writes: "Estas páginas son un fragmento de las 'Memorias Amables,' que ya muy viejo empezó a escribir en la emigración el Marqués de Bradomín. Un Don Juan admirable. ¡El más admirable tal vez! Era feo, católico y sentimental" (*Sonata de primavera y sonata de estío* [Madrid: Espasa-Calpe, 1963], 8). Toward the end of the *Winter Sonata* Bradomín is again called: "el más admirable de los Don Juanes: Feo, católico y sentimental," by his aunt (*Sonata de otoño y sonata de invierno* [Madrid: Espasa-Calpe, 1963], 174).
11. *Sonata de primavera y sonata de estío,* 107.
12. Ibid., 150.
13. Ibid., 81.
14. Nora, "La novela española," 61–62.
15. Throughout the *Sonatas* and even in other works, Valle has a fondness for the name María, with the result that María Remedios, María

Isabel, María Rosario, María Fernanda, María de la Concepción, and others are frequent ones.

16. *Aromas de leyenda* and *El pasajero* were published in 1907 and 1920 respectively. Eventually they appeared together with *La pipa de kif* (1919) in a volume titled *Claves líricas* in 1946.

17. Harold L. Boudreau, "Valle-Inclán's Return to the Novel: 1926–1936," in *Ramón del Valle-Inclán,* ed. Zahareas, 695.

18. María Dolores Lado, "La trilogía de *La guerra carlista,*" in ibid., 340.

19. "No tenía otro hijo en el mundo, pero mejor lo quiero aquí muerto, como lo vedes todos agora, que como yo lo vide esta tarde, crucificando a Dios Nuestro Señor," says the mother to Don Juan Manuel Montenegro in *Los cruzados de la causa* (*La Guerra Carlista* [Madrid: Aguilar, 1970], 51).

20. Julián Marías, *Valle Inclán en "El Ruedo Ibérico"* (Buenos Aires, 1967), 17.

21. Boudreau, "Valle-Inclan's Return," 695.

22. Cited in ibid., 696.

23. Ibid.

24. For further elaboration of the cabalistic scheme and structure of this novel see Oldrich Belic, *La estructura narrativa de Tirano Banderas* (Madrid: Editora Nacional, 1968).

25. Cited by Boudreau, "Valle-Inclan's Return," 696.

26. Verity Smith, *Ramón del Valle Inclán* (New York, 1973), 128.

27. Harold L. Boudreau, "Continuity in the *Ruedo Ibérico,*" in *Ramón del Valle-Inclán,* ed. Zahareas, 777.

28. Harold L. Boudreau, "The Moral Comment of the *Ruedo Ibérico,*" in ibid., 795.

Chapter Five

1. José Ortega y Gasset, "Sobre el arte de Baroja," in *El Espectador: Antología,* ed. Paulino Garagorri (Madrid: Alianza Editorial, 1980), 25–30.

2. *Tinieblas en las cumbres,* ed. Andrés Amorós (Madrid: Castalia, 1971), 7–8.

3. *Troteras y danzaderas,* ed. Andrés Amorós (Madrid: Castalia, 1972), 26.

4. *Obras completas,* ed. José García Mercadal, vol. 1 (Madrid: Aguilar, 1963), lxix–lxxi.

5. *Tinieblas,* ed., Amorós, 15.

6. *Troteras,* ed., Amorós, 25.

7. Ibid.

8. Nora, *La novela española,* 495. Nora Cites, among others, Jean Cassou and César Barja as critics who share his opinion.

9. Ibid.

10. Ibid., 480.

11. Andrés Amorós, *La novela intelectual de Ramón Pérez de Ayala* (Madrid, 1972), 83.

12. This title appears only in the second edition of *La pata de la raposa.*

13. Marguerite C. Rand, *Ramón Pérez de Ayala* (New York, 1971), 75.

14. Amorós, *La novela intelectual,* 206–9.

15. Another volume, published in 1924, *El ombligo del mundo,* was also subtitled "Novelas poématicas." It contained five stories: "Grano de pimienta y mil perdones," "La triste Adriana," "Don Rodrigo y Don Recaredo," "Clib," and "El profesor auxiliar."

16. Gonzalo Sobejano, *Nietzsche en España* (Madrid, 1967), 595.

17. *Prometeo, Luz de domingo, La caída de los limones* (Buenos Aires: Losada, 1967), 88.

18. Rand, *Ramón Pérez de Ayala,* 89.

19. See for example, T. R. Ybarra, "An Ayala Novel: *Belarmino y Apolonio,*" *New York Times Book Review,* 6 March 1921, p. 24.

20. Amorós, *La novela intelectual,* 321.

21. Rand, *Ramón Pérez de Ayala,* 112.

Chapter Six

1. José Ortega y Gasset, "*El obispo leproso,* novela, por Gabriel Miró," in *Obras completas,* vol. 3 (Madrid: Biblioteca Nueva, 1932), 544–50.

2. Juan Guerrero, "Unas cartas de Gabriel Miró," *Cuadernos de Literatura Contemporánea* 5–6 (1942):219.

3. Quoted as "No olvido nunca mis largas temporadas pasadas en la enfermería de un colegio de Jesuítas, desde cuyas ventanas he sentido las primeras tristezas estéticas, viendo en los crepúsculos los valles apagados y las cumbres de las sierras aún encendidas de sol" (Andrés González Blanco, *Los Contemporáneos,* 1st ser. [Paris: Garnier, 1906], 290).

4. Ibid., 290.

5. Ricardo L. Landeira, *Gabriel Miró: Trilogía de Sigüenza* (Chapel Hill, N.C., 1972), 15.

6. González Blanco, *Los Contemporáneos,* 291.

7. Landeira, *Gabriel Miró,* 17.

8. On 1927 and 1929 the majority of the Academy's membership voted to exclude Miró (ibid., 18).

9. Quoted in Ricardo Landeira, *An Annotated Bibliography of Gabriel Miró (1900–1978)* (Lincoln, 1978), 4.

10. *Obras Completas,* 4th ed. (Madrid, 1961), 1196.

11. Nora, *La novela española,* 442.

12. Juan Chabás, *Literatura española contemporánea* (Havana: Cultural, 1952), 295.

13. Northrup Frye, "Fictional Modes and Forms," in *Approaches to the Novel,* ed. Robert Scholes (San Francisco: Chandler Publishing Co., 1961), 23–42.

14. These and subsequent pages refer to the 1961 edition of *Obras completas.*

15. Ricardo Landeira, "La narrativa autobiográfica de Gabriel Miró," in *La novela lírica,* ed. Darío Villanueva, 2 vols. (Madrid, 1983), 1:262.[11]

16. Ibid., 262.

17. Landeira, *Trilogía de Sigüenza,* 35.

18. For a more detailed study of the genesis of this work see my *Gabriel Miró: Trilogía de Sigüenza,* 60–113.

19. Nora, *La novela española,* 456.

20. Ibid., 462.

21. Yvette E. Miller, "Illusion of Reality and Narrative Technique in Gabriel Miró's Oleza-Orihuela Novels: *Nuestro Padre San Daniel* and *El obispo leproso,*" in *Critical Essays on Gabriel Miró,* ed. Ricardo Landeira (Ann Arbor: Society of Spanish and Spanish-American Studies, 1979), 58.

Chapter Seven

1. While Antonio Machado is universally acknowledged as the foremost poet of the Generation of 1898, it is not so widely known that he wrote several plays, most of them in collaboration with his brother Manuel. Of a lyrical nature, they were received as poorly by the public as by the critics. Their best are *Las adelfas* (1928), *La Lola se va a los puertos* (1930), and *La duquesa de Benamejí* (1932).

2. Landeira, *Ramiro de Maeztu,* 132-33.

3. "Puntualizaciones de 'Taurus' sobre el supuesto plagio de *La cara de Dios,*" *La Voz de Galicia,* 14 February 1973.

4. *La cara de Dios,* ed. Domingo García Sabell (Madrid: Taurus, 1972).

5. José Ortega y Gasset, "Azorín: primores de lo vulgar," in *El Espectador,* vol. 2 (Madrid: Revista de Occidente, 1963), 57–116.

6. Luis S. Granjel, "Azorín, novelista," *Cuadernos Hispanoamericanos* 226–27 (October–November 1968):182–91.

7. Nora, *La novela española,* 231–60.

8. *La voluntad,* ed. E. Inman Fox (Madrid: Editorial Castalia, 1968), 9–46.

9. Kathleen M. Glenn, *Azorín* (Boston, 1981).

10. Robert E. Lott, "Sobre el método narrativo y el estilo en las novelas de Azorín," *Cuadernos Hispanoamericanos* 226–27 (October–November 1968):192–219.

11. Leon Livingstone, *Tema y forma en las novelas de Azorín* (Madrid, 1970).

12. Some of Azorín's first journalistic publications appeared in Blasco's radical *El Pueblo* in early 1905.

13. Guillermo Díaz Plaja, "El teatro de Azorín," *Cuadernos de Literatura Contemporánea* 16–17 (1947):369–87.

14. Glenn, *Azorín*, 126–29; Lott, "Sobre el método narrativo," 208–14.

15. Ortega y Gasset, "Azorín," 57–144.

16. Nora cites Max Aub and Torrente Ballester as prime examples of the negative critical reaction R. León continues to elicit (*La novela española*, 310).

17. Two recent books may signal an end to the critical silence that has surrounded Fernández Flórez and his novel: Albert Mature, *Wenceslao Fernández Flórez y su novela* (Mexico City, 1968), and José Carlos Mainer, *Análisis de una insatisfacción: Las novelas de W. Fernández Flórez* (Madrid, 1975).

18. Mainer, *Análisis*, 32.

19. Ibid., 37.

20. Nora, *La novela española*, 7–39.

21. Mainer, *Análisis*, 25.

22. Nora, *La novela española*, 186.

Selected Bibliography

Owing to the authors' enormous production, as well as to the unwieldy amount of material written about them, I have not attempted a total compilation. Instead, I have chosen to include in the primary sources section only novels, collected works, and book-length bibliographies from which the reader can gather a more complete reference regarding any topic or work of interest. In the secondary sources section I have limited the selected entries, except in very few cases, to book-length studies or monographs published separately.

PRIMARY SOURCES

1. Bibliographies

Fernández, Pelayo H. *Bibliografía crítica de Miguel de Unamuno*. Madrid: José Porrúa Turanzas, 1976.
Landeira, Ricardo. *An Annotated Bibliography of Gabriel Miró (1900–1978)*. Lincoln: University of Nebraska, Society of Spanish and Spanish-American Studies, 1978.
Lima, Robert. *An Annotated Bibliography of Ramón del Valle-Inclán*. University Park: Pennsylvania State University Libraries, 1972.
Saínz de Bujada, Fernando. *Guía bibliográfica de Azorín*. Madrid: Revista de Occidente, 1974.

2. Collected Works

Vicente Blasco Ibáñez
Obras completas. 11 vols. Valencia: Prometeo, 1925.
Obras completas. 3 vols. Madrid: Aguilar, 1946.

Miguel de Unamuno
Obras completas. 16 vols. Madrid: Afrodisio Aguado, 1958–64.

Pío Baroja
Obras completas. 8 vols. Madrid: Biblioteca Nueva, 1946–51.

Ramón del Valle Inclán
Obras completas de don Ramón del Valle Inclán. 2 vols. Madrid: Editorial Plenitud, 1952–54.
"Opera Omnia" de don Ramón del Valle Inclán. 29 vols. Madrid: Editorial Rúa Nueva-Talleres Tipográficos Rivadeneyra, 1941–43; Madrid: Editorial Plenitud–Gráficas Clemares, 1954–.

Ramón Pérez de Ayala
Obras completas. 4 vols. Madrid: Aguilar, 1964–69. Incomplete.

Gabriel Miró
Obras completas. 4th ed. Madrid: Biblioteca Nueva 1961.

José Martínez Ruiz, Azorín
Obras completas. 9 vols. Madrid: Aguilar, 1959–63.

3. Novels (First Editions)

Vicente Blasco Ibáñez
Arroz y tartana. Valencia: F. Sempere y Cía., 1894.
Flor de mayo. Valencia: F. Sempere y Cía., 1896.
La barraca. Valencia: F. Sempere y Cía., 1898.
Entre naranjos. Valencia: F. Sempere y Cía., 1900.
Sónnica la cortesana. Valencia: F. Sempere y Cía., 1901.
Cañas y barro. Valencia: Sempere, 1902.
La catedral. Valencia: Prometeo, 1903.
El intruso. Valencia: Prometeo, 1904.
La bodega. Valencia: Sempere y Cía., 1905.
La horda. Valencia: Sempere y Cía., 1905.
La maja desnuda. Valencia: F. Sempere y Cía., 1906.
Sangre y arena. Valencia: F. Sempere y Cía., 1908.
Los muertos mandan. Valencia: F. Sempere y Cía., 1908.
Luna Benamor. Valencia: F. Sempere y Cía., 1909.
Los Argonautas. Valencia: Prometeo, 1914.
Los cuatro jinetes del Apocalipsis. Valencia: Prometeo, 1916.
Mare Nostrum. Valencia: Prometeo, 1917.
Los enemigos de la mujer. Valencia: Prometeo, 1919.
La tierra de todos. Valencia: Prometeo, 1921.
El paraíso de las mujeres. Valencia: Prometeo, 1922.
La reina Calafia. Valencia: Prometeo, 1923.
El papa del mar. Valencia: Prometeo, 1925.
A los pies de Venus. Valencia: Prometeo, 1926.
En busca del Gran Kan. Valencia: Albatros, 1929.
El caballero de la Virgen. Valencia: Prometeo, 1929.

El fantasma de las alas de oro. Valencia: Prometeo, 1930.
La voluntad de vivir. Barcelona: Editorial Planeta, 1953.

Miguel de Unamuno

Paz en la guerra. Madrid: Fe, 1897.
Amor y pedagogía. Barcelona: Heinrich, 1902.
Niebla. Madrid: Renacimiento, 1914.
Abel Sánchez. Madrid: Renacimiento, 1917.
Tres novelas ejemplares y un prólogo. Madrid: Calpe, 1920.
La tía Tula. Madrid: Renacimiento, 1921.
Cómo se hace una novela. Buenos Aires, 1927.
San Manuel Bueno, mártir y tres historias más. Madrid: Espasa-Calpe, 1933.

Pío Baroja

Vidas sombrías. Madrid: Miguel de Pereda, 1900.
La casa de Aizgorri. Bilbao: Fermín Herrán, 1900.
Aventuras, inventos y mixtificaciones de Silvestre Paradox. Madrid: Rodríguez Serra, 1901.
Camino de perfección. Madrid: Rodríguez Serra, 1902.
El mayorazgo de Labraz. Barcelona: Heinrich y Cía., 1903.
La busca. Madrid: Fernando Fe, 1904.
Mala hierba. Madrid: Fernando Fe, 1904.
El tablado de Arlequín. Valencia: Sempere, 1904.
Aurora roja. Madrid: Fernando Fe, 1904.
La feria de los discretos. Madrid: Fernando Fe, 1905.
Paradox, rey. Madrid: Hernando, 1906.
Los últimos románticos. Madrid: Hernando, 1906.
Las tragedias grotescas. Madrid: Hernando, 1906.
La dama errante. Madrid: Hernando, 1908.
La ciudad de la niebla. Madrid: Hernando, 1909.
Zalacaín el aventurero. Barcelona: Domenech, 1909.
César o nada. Madrid: Renacimiento, 1910.
Las inquietudes de Shanti Andía. Madrid: Renacimiento, 1911.
El árbol de la ciencia. Madrid: Renacimiento, 1911.
El mundo es ansí. Madrid: Renacimiento, 1912.
El aprendiz de conspirador. Madrid: Renacimiento, 1913.
El escuadrón del Brigante. Madrid: Renacimiento, 1913.
Los caminos del mundo. Madrid: Renacimiento, 1914.
Los recursos de la astucia. Madrid: Renacimiento, 1915.
La ruta del aventurero. Madrid: Renacimiento, 1916.
Juventud, egolatría. Madrid: Caro Raggio, 1917.
La veleta de Gastizar. Madrid: Caro Raggio, 1918.

Los contrastes de la vida. Madrid: Caro Raggio, 1920.

La sensualidad pervertida. Madrid: Caro Raggio, 1920.

El sabor de la venganza. Madrid: Caro Raggio, 1921.

Las furias. Madrid: Caro Raggio, 1921.

La leyenda de Jaun de Alzate. Madrid: Caro Raggio, 1922.

El laberinto de las sirenas. Madrid: Caro Raggio, 1923.

Las figuras de cera. Madrid: Caro Raggio, 1924.

La nave de los locos. Madrid: Caro Raggio, 1925.

Las veleidades de la fortuna. Madrid: Caro Raggio, 1926.

El gran torbellino del mundo. Madrid: Caro Raggio, 1926.

Los amores tardíos. Madrid: Caro Raggio, 1927.

Las mascaradas sangrientas. Madrid: Caro Raggio, 1927.

Humano enigma. Madrid: Caro Raggio, 1928.

La senda dolorosa. Madrid: Caro Raggio, 1928.

Los pilotos de altura. Madrid: Caro Raggio, 1929.

La estrella del Capitán Chimista. Madrid: Caro Raggio, 1930.

Aviraneta o la vida de un conspirador. Madrid: Espasa-Calpe, 1931.

La familia de Errotacho. Madrid: Espasa-Calpe, 1932.

El cabo de las tormentas. Madrid: Espasa-Calpe, 1932.

Los visionarios. Madrid: Espasa-Calpe, 1932.

Juan Van Halen, el oficial aventurero. Madrid: Espasa-Calpe, 1933.

Las noches del Buen Retiro. Madrid: Espasa-Calpe, 1934.

El cura de Monleón. Madrid: Espasa-Calpe, 1936.

El caballero de Erlaiz. Madrid: La Nave, 1943.

El puente de las ánimas. Madrid: La Nave, 1945.

El Hotel del Cisne. Madrid: Biblioteca Nueva, 1946.

Los enigmáticos. Madrid: Biblioteca Nueva, 1948.

Ramón del Valle Inclán

Sonata de otoño. Madrid: A. Pérez, 1902.

Sonata de estío. Madrid: A. Marzo, 1903.

Sonata de primavera. Madrid: A. Marzo, 1904.

Flor de santidad. Madrid: A. Marzo, 1904.

Sonata de invierno. Madrid: Tipografía de la Revista de Archivos, Bibliotecas y Museos, 1905.

Los cruzados de la causa. Madrid: Imprenta de Balgañón y Moreno, 1908.

El resplandor de la hoguera. Madrid: P. Fernández, 1908–9.

Gerifaltes de antaño. Madrid: P. Fernández, 1908–9.

Tirano Banderas. Madrid: Sucesores de Rivadeneyra, 1926.

La corte de los milagros. Madrid: Rivadeneyra, 1927.

Viva mi dueño. Madrid: Rivadeneyra, 1928.

Baza de espadas. Barcelona: AHR, 1958.

Ramón Pérez de Ayala
Tinieblas en las cumbres. Madrid: Fernando Fe, 1907.
Sonreía. Madrid: Tip. Blas, 1909.
A.M.D.G. Madrid: Imprenta Artística Española, 1910.
La pata de la raposa. Madrid: Biblioteca Renacimiento, 1913.
Troteras y danzaderas. Madrid: Biblioteca Renacimiento, 1913.
Prometeo, Luz de domingo, La caída de los Limones. Madrid: Imprenta Clásica Española, 1916.
Belarmino y Apolonio. Madrid: Calleja, 1921.
Luna de miel, luna de hiel. Madrid: Mundo Latino, 1923.
Los trabajos de Urbano y Simona. Madrid: Mundo Latino, 1923.
El ombligo del mundo. Madrid: Rivadeneyra, Renacimiento, 1924.
Bajo el signo de Artemisa. Madrid: Renacimiento, 1924.
Tigre Juan. Madrid: Pueyo, 1926.
El curandero de su honra. Madrid: Pueyo, 1926.
Justicia. Madrid: Ed. unknown, 1928.

Gabriel Miró
La mujer de Ojeda. Alicante: Imp. Juan José Carratalá, 1901.
Hilván de escenas. Alicante: Imp. Luis Esplá, 1903.
Del vivir. Alicante: Imp. Luis Esplá, 1904.
La novela de mi amigo. Alicante: Imp. Luis Esplá, 1908.
Las cerezas del cementerio. Barcelona: Ed. E. Domenech, 1910.
Del huerto provinciano: Nómada. Barcelona: Ed. E. Domenech, 1912.
El abuelo del rey. Barcelona: Editorial Ibérica, 1915.
Dentro del cercado: La palma rota. Barcelona: Ed. E. Domenech, 1916.
Libro de Sigüenza. Barcelona: Ed. E. Domenech, 1917.
Nuestro Padre San Daniel. Madrid: Ed. Atenea, 1921.
Niño y grande. Madrid: Ed. Atenea, 1922.
El obispo leproso. Madrid: Ed. Biblioteca Nueva, 1926.
Años y leguas. Madrid: Ed. Biblioteca Nueva, 1928.

José Martínez Ruiz, Azorín
Diario de un enfermo. Madrid: Establecimiento Tipográfico de Ricardo Fe, 1901.
La voluntad. Barcelona: Henrich y Cía., 1902.
Antonio Azorín. Madrid: Viuda de Rodríguez Serra, 1903.
Las confesiones de un pequeño filósofo. Madrid: Librería de Fernando Fe, 1904.
El licenciado Vidriera visto por Azorín (Tomás Rueda). Madrid: Residencia de Estudiantes, 1915.
Don Juan. Madrid: Caro Raggio, 1922.
Doña Inés. Madrid: Caro Raggio, 1925.
Félix Vargas (El caballero inactual). Madrid: Biblioteca Nueva, 1928.
Superrealismo (El libro de Levante). Madrid: Biblioteca Nueva, 1929.

Pueblo. Madrid: Biblioteca Nueva, 1930.
El escritor. Madrid: Espasa-Calpe, 1942.
El enfermo. Madrid: Adán, 1943.
Capricho. Madrid: Espasa-Calpe, 1943.
La isla sin aurora. Barcelona: Destino, 1944.
María Fontán. Madrid: Espasa-Calpe, 1944.
Salvadora de Olbena. Zaragoza: Cronos, 1944.

Benjamín Jarnés
El profesor inútil. Madrid: Espasa-Calpe, 1926.
El convidado de papel. Madrid: Historia Nueva, 1928.
Locura y muerte de nadie. Madrid: Ediciones Oriente, 1929.
Paula y Paulita. Madrid: Revista de Occidente, 1929.
Teoría del zumbel. Madrid: Espasa-Calpe, 1930.
Viviana y Merlín: Leyenda. Madrid: Ediciones Ulises, 1930.
Escenas junto a la muerte. Madrid: Espasa-Calpe, 1931.
Lo rojo y lo azul: Homenaje a Stendahl. Madrid: Espasa-Calpe, 1932.
Don Alvaro o la fuerza del tino. Madrid: Editores Reunidos, 1936.
Venus dinámica. Mexico City: Editorial Proa, 1943.
Constelación de Friné. Mexico City: Editorial Proa, 1944.

SECONDARY SOURCES

General
Díaz Plaja, Guillermo. *Modernismo frente a Noventa y Ocho.* Madrid: Espasa-Calpe, 1966. Contrasting looks at the members of this generation, their writings and aesthetics.
Eoff, Sherman H. *The Modern Spanish Novel.* New York: New York University Press, 1961. Comparative essays on Blasco, Baroja, and Unamuno, among other Spanish novelists, and their European contemporaries.
Granjel, Luis. *La generación literaria del 98.* Salamanca: Anaya, 1971. More on this generation by an expert on the subject among whose previous works are *Panorama de la Generación del 98* (Madrid: Guadarrama, 1959) and *Baroja y otras figuras del 98* (Madrid: Guadarrama, 1960).
Laín Entralgo, Pedro. *La generación del Noventa y Ocho.* Madrid: Espasa-Calpe, 1963. The best starting point on the Generation of 1898.
Nora, Eugenio G. de. *La novela española contemporánea (1898–1927).* 3 vols. Madrid: Editorial Gredos, 1963. The most comprehensive (1898–1960) and reliable study on the novel of this period.

Sobejano, Gonzalo. *Nietzsche en España.* Madrid: Editorial Gredos, 1967. Indispensable treatise on this philosopher's influence from Valera to Cela. Well documented and argued.

Villanueva, Darío, ed. *La novela lírica,* 2 vols. Madrid: Taurus, 1983. Excellent collection of essays on Azorín, Miró, Pérez de Ayala, and Jarnés.

Vicente Blasco Ibáñez

Day, A. Grove, and Edgar C. Knowlton, Jr. *Vicente Blasco Ibáñez.* New York: Twayne Publishers, 1972. Basic life and works volume.

Gasco Contell, Emilio. *Genio y figura de Blasco Ibáñez, agitador, aventurero y novelista.* Madrid: Afrodisio Aguado, 1957. Traditional biography written by a friend of the novelist.

León Roca, J. L. *Vicente Blasco Ibáñez.* Valencia: Prometeo, 1967. The last and most useful life and works volume written in Spanish.

Martínez de la Riva, Ramón. *Blasco Ibáñez, su vida, su obra, su muerte, sus mejores páginas.* Madrid: Mundo Latino, 1929. Includes a bit of everything. Not bad as a sample of Blasco's life and writings.

Pitollet, Camilo. *Vicente Blasco Ibáñez: sus novelas y la novela de su vida.* Valencia: Prometeo, 1921. The work of an admirer, lacking scholarly rigor.

Miguel de Unamuno

Blanco Aguinaga, Carlos. *El Unamuno contemplativo.* Barcelona: Editorial Laia, 1975. An original book looking at Unamuno's other side.

Clavería, Carlos. *Temas de Unamuno.* Madrid: Gredos, 1953. Contains perceptive essays on the Cain and Abel theme among other important Unamunian preoccupations.

Ferrater Mora, José. *Unamuno: Bosquejo de una filosofía.* Buenos Aires: Editorial Sudamericana, 1957. A good analysis of Unamuno's philosophy of tragedy.

García Blanco, Manuel. *En torno a Unamuno.* Madrid: Taurus, 1965. Various essays of indispensable value by a dedicated Unamuno scholar and archivist.

Marías, Julián. *Miguel de Unamuno.* Madrid: Espasa-Calpe, 1961. A comprehensive look at Unamuno's literature and philosophy.

Nozick, Martin. *Miguel de Unamuno.* New York: Twayne Publishers, 1971. The best English language study on Unamuno. Heavily weighted toward the author's philosophy.

Salcedo, Emilio. *Vida de Don Miguel.* Salamanca: Anaya, 1964. Entertaining and informative biography. The best of its kind in either English or Spanish.

Pío Baroja

Arbó, Sebastián Juan. *Pío Baroja y su tiempo*. Barcelona: Planeta, 1963. Voluminous work on every aspect of Baroja's life and several of his contemporaries. Lacks scholarly care.

Baeza, Fernando, ed. *Baroja y su mundo*. 3 vols. Madrid: Arion, 1961. Important work whose essays dwell on biographical and critical themes. It contains also a large bibliography.

Caro Baroja, Julio. *La soledad de Pío Baroja*. Mexico City: Ed. Pío Caro Baroja, 1953. Baroja's last years as told by his nephew.

Fox, E. Inman. "Baroja and Schopenhauer." *Revue de littérature comparée* 37 (1963):350–59. Excellent article on *El árbol de la ciencia* and Baroja's pessimism.

García Mercadal, José, ed. *Baroja en el banquillo*. 2 vols. Zaragoza: Librería General, 1947–48. A critical anthology of Spanish and foreign criticism.

Nallim, Carlos Orlando. *El problema de la novela en Pío Baroja*. Mexico City: Ateneo, 1964. Analyses and plot summaries of the important novels.

Patt, Beatrice P. *Pío Baroja*. New York: Twayne Publishers, 1971. Basic life and works volume.

Pérez Ferrero, Miguel. *Pío Baroja en su rincón*. San Sebastián: Internacional, 1941. Baroja's best and most constant biographer, also author of *Vida de Pío Baroja* (Barcelona: Destino, 1960).

Ramón del Valle Inclán

Díaz Plaja, Guillermo. *Las estéticas de Valle Inclán*. Madrid: Gredos, 1965. Study of Valle's art in its three distinct stages.

Fernández Almagro, Melchor. *Vida y literatura de Valle Inclán*. Madrid: Nacional, 1943. Long on his life, short on his works.

Madrid, Francisco. *La vida altiva de Valle Inclán*. Buenos Aires: Poseidon, 1943. Biography and extracts of interviews and lectures.

Marías, Julián. *Valle Inclán en "El Ruedo Ibérico."* Buenos Aires: Columba, 1967. Brief look at Valle's symbiosis of history and fiction in his last three novels.

Smith, Verity. *Ramón del Valle Inclán*. New York: Twayne Publishers, 1973. Basic life and works volume.

———. *Valle Inclán: Tirano Banderas*. London: Grant & Cutler, 1971. Detailed analysis of Valle's masterpiece novel.

Speratti Pinero, Emma Susana. *De "Sonata de otoño" al Esperpento*. London: Támesis, 1968. Classical study of Valle's aesthetics. Indispensable.

Ynduráin, Francisco. *Valle Inclán: Tres estudios*. Santander: La Isla de los Ratones, 1969. Three essays on *La corte de los milagros* and *Viva mi dueño*.

Zahareas, Anthony, ed. *Ramón del Valle Inclán: An Appraisal of His Life and Works.* New York: Las América, 1968. The best single-volume collection of essays on Valle's life, writings, and aesthetics.

Zamora, Vicente. *Las Sonatas de Ramón del Valle Inclán.* Madrid: Gredos, 1955. A good study of Valle's modernistic period.

Ramón Pérez de Ayala

Amorós, Andrés. *Vida y literatura en "Troteras y danzaderas."* Madrid: Castalia, 1973. Who is really who in this roman á clef, plus more on Ayala's Madrid.

———. *La novela intelectual de Ramón Pérez de Ayala.* Madrid: Gredos: 1972. A solid work of scholarship by Ayala's most active critic.

Rand, Marguerite C. *Ramón Pérez de Ayala.* New York: Twayne Publishers, 1971. Basic life and works book.

Reinink, K. W. *Algunos aspectos literarios y lingüísticos de la obra de Don Ramón Pérez de Ayala.* The Hague: G. B. Van Goor Zonen's, 1959. A general study of Ayala and his literary relations.

Urrutia, Norma. *De "Troteras" a "Tigre Juan"—dos grandes temas de Ramón Pérez de Ayala.* Madrid: Insula, 1960. One of the first, good, comprehensive books on Ayala's novels.

Weber, Frances W. *The Literary Perspectives of Ramón Pérez de Ayala.* Chapel Hill: University of North Carolina Press, 1966. Perceptive look at characters and narrators in Ayala's most important novels.

Gabriel Miró

King, Edmund L. "Gabriel Miró y 'el mundo según es.' " *Papeles de Son Armadans* 62 (May 1962):121–42. A compact essay on Miró's aesthetics and ethics.

Landeira, Ricardo, ed. *Critical Essays on Gabriel Miró.* Ann Arbor: Society of Spanish and Spanish-American Studies, 1979. A collection of essays on Miró's fiction by his best-known critics.

———. *Gabriel Miró: Trilogía de Sigüenza.* Chapel Hill, N.C.: Estudios de Hispanófila, 1972. A detailed analysis of the three Sigüenza works.

Ramos, Vicente. *El mundo de Gabriel Miró.* Madrid: Gredos, 1970. The most comprehensive work by Miró's best-known living critic.

Minor Novelists

Bernstein, J. S. *Benjamín Jarnés.* Boston: Twayne Publishers, 1972. Basic life and works volume.

Bretz, Mary Lee. *Concha Espina.* Boston: Twayne Publishers, 1980. A basic life and works study.

Diego, Gerardo. *Centenario de Concha Espina.* Santander, 1970. Essays on the novelist and selections from her works.

Glenn, Kathleen M. *Azorín*. Boston: Twayne Publishers, 1981. Basic life and works study.

Granell, Manuel. *Estética de Azorín*. Madrid: Biblioteca Nueva, 1949. Among the topics discussed are Azorín's obsession with time and diminute reality.

Livingstone, Leon. *Tema y forma en las novelas de Azorín*. Madrid: Gredos, 1970. The best full-length work on Azorín's narrative fiction.

Mainer, José Carlos. *Análisis de una insatisfacción: Las novelas de W. Fernández Flórez*. Madrid: Castalia, 1975. A doctoral dissertation with invaluable data.

Martínez Cachero, José Maria. *Las novelas de Azorín*. Madrid: Insula, 1960. A general commentary on the writing of novels by Azorín.

Mature, Albert. *Wenceslao Fernández Flórez y su novela*. Mexico City: Studium, 1968. Good general work whose chronological approach is enlightening.

Maza, Josefina de la. *Vida de mi madre, Concha Espina*. Madrid: Magisterio Español, 1960. A good biography with predictable flaws.

Mellizo, Carlos, ed. *Homenaje a Azorín*. Laramie: University of Wyoming, Department of Modern and Classical Languages, 1973. Collection of essays of varying quality.

Index